Martin Eichelberger
MD
PHOENIX, ARIZONA
AUGUST 27, 1999

The two broke free. One vanished and
the other landed on the highest bush.
The colors were brilliant, focused on
a few small areas of the wings. There
was a strange motion at the fan end
of the wings and for a moment I
thought I was seeing some strange replication.
What I was seeing were the sets of wings
rubbed vertically together and two small
black streamers waving up and down.
The butterfly stayed put and I inched
close to it to begin drawing. One
portion of a wing drummed and the thing
fluttered into the air, in a tight conflict
with another butterfly. I figured they were
also vying for a spot where receptive females will arrive. The
... must be this bush, which I know only is the bush I will
grudgingly walk through if given a choice between it and a
... later Irwin told me it was in the same family with the tomato,
... a capitate stamen twisting a small green ball above the pistils, which
... hard to generally for small petals.
... climbed down the other side after scanning the terrain for Irwin.

Wild
Mustard

GRANDCANYON
TIME BELOW THE RIM

TEXT BY CRAIG CHILDS   PHOTOGRAPHS BY GARY LADD

ACKNOWLEDGMENTS

Author Craig Childs, photographer Gary Ladd, and the editors of *Grand Canyon: Time Below the Rim* gratefully acknowledge the many individuals, companies, and organizations whose contributions enhanced this book. Over many months, they shared knowledge, gave logistical support, and assisted us unstintingly in developing this book.

Rangers and other specialists of the National Park Service at Grand Canyon National Park and staff members of the Grand Canyon Association offered technical advice, in-depth information, and logistical help. Their willingness, enthusiasm, and insights helped immeasurably.

The Grand Canyon's river-running community, from individual adventure companies to the members of Grand Canyon River Guides, exerted special effort to help Gary and his camera reach all parts of the Canyon. The revealing diversity of his Canyon portraits is the colorful result.

For their generosity, we recognize: Arizona Raft Adventures, Canyon Explorations/Canyon Expeditions, Outdoors Unlimited, and Professional River Outfitters, all in Flagstaff, Arizona; Arizona River Runners of Phoenix, Arizona; Colorado River & Trail Expeditions and Western River Expeditions, both of Salt Lake City, Utah; Diamond River Adventures and Wilderness River Adventures, both of Page, Arizona; Grand Canyon Expeditions Company of Kanab, Utah; Hatch River Expeditions of Vernal, Utah; OARS/Grand Canyon Dories of Altaville, California; and Tour West of Orem, Utah.

Finally, OARS/Grand Canyon Dories hauled Craig down the Canyon's entire length for the water-logged perspective necessary for Chapter Six, *Wooden Boats*. On that trip, two passengers known only as Shawn and Roger saw the author's notes get flung into the rapids and shouted an alert in time for him to dive in and retrieve them. To Shawn, Roger, and all the rest who became friends and partners in our adventure, many thanks.

Opposite: The Colorado River tumbles through a maze of boulders at the head of 164 Mile Rapids at the mouth of Tuckup Canyon on a March morning.

Prepared by the Book Division of *Arizona Highways*® magazine, a monthly publication of the Arizona Department of Transportation.

Book Designer: MARY WINKELMAN VELGOS
Photography Editor: PETER ENSENBERGER
Copy Editors: CHARLES BURKHART AND EVELYN HOWELL
Book Editor: BOB ALBANO

Publisher: Nina M. La France
Managing Editor: Bob Albano
Associate Editor: Evelyn Howell
Art Director: Mary Winkelman Velgos
Photography Director: Peter Ensenberger
Production Director: Cindy Mackey

Library of Congress Catalog Card Number 98-87499. ISBN 0-916179-78-8

ARIZONA HIGHWAYS BOOKS

CRAIG CHILDS

The backcountry — generally in Arizona or Utah, mostly in deserts — is Craig Childs' home for nine months each year as he explores and conducts research for projects. For this book, he spent 120 days exploring the backcountry of the Grand Canyon.

Writing is the byproduct of Craig's fascination with severe landscapes, and with the ancient peoples who once inhabited them. Since his teens he has worked as a river guide and field instructor in the Southwest. After receiving a bachelor's degree in journalism and women's studies, and working on a community newspaper in Ouray, Colorado, he earned a master's degree in desert studies from Prescott College in Prescott, Arizona. Now, he teaches field courses for the college.

He has written for numerous publications, including *Arizona Highways, Audubon, Sierra, Backpacker*, and the *Alligator Juniper* literary journal. In 1993 he won a nature writing competition sponsored by *Sierra*. He previously published two books, *Stone Desert: A Naturalist's Exploration of Canyonlands National Park* and *Crossing Paths: Uncommon Encounters with Animals in the Wild*.

GARY LADD

Gary Ladd has been exploring and photographing the Grand Canyon since 1964, when he hiked a short distance on the Bright Angel Trail with his parents and siblings.

Since then, he has ventured on some 60 backpacking trips and scores of shorter hikes into the Canyon and its tributaries. On one series of treks, he followed trails from Lees Ferry to Lava Falls covering about two-thirds of the Canyon's length. Likewise, he engaged in several trips hiking from Cameron, Arizona, down the Little Colorado River to its confluence with the Colorado, and from there to Elves Chasm, about 50 miles downriver.

He embarked on his first Colorado River trip at Lees Ferry in 1970. Since then, he has rowed his dory — the *Tatahotso* — through the Canyon several times.

Despite an intimate familiarity, he writes, "No matter how well someone knows it, the Canyon forever presents surprises awaiting discovery."

Gary, a frequent photographic and story contributor to *Arizona Highways*, specializes in large-format photography supplemented with the 35mm format. He lives in Page, Arizona.

Opposite: From a rim of Redwall limestone, a cottontop cactus watches the Colorado River swirl towards Tatahatso Point. The site where a Marble Canyon dam once was envisioned lies two miles downstream.

Following panel: The azure waters of the Little Colorado River, which flows westward across much of northern Arizona, surge toward an early-morning meeting with the master stream.

CONTENTS

Most of the illustrations accompanying these six chapters were drawn by Craig Childs in a journal he keeps when he explores the backcountry. He drew a few after his return from the Grand Canyon. Gary Ladd's photographs accompanying the chapters depict the areas in which the author trekked. But the two did not travel together in the Canyon.

Photographer Gary Ladd wrote the introductions for each of his six Grand Canyon portfolios and assisted in the writing of captions. The first four portfolios progress geographically from the Canyon's start to its end. The term "River Mile" frequently is used in establishing reference points. River Mile 0, the Canyon's start, is at Lees Ferry. River Mile 277 is at the upper end of Lake Mead.

CRAIG CHILDS

EVEN THE GRAND CANYON HAS AN EDGE. MADE OF LIMESTONE AND SOLID TO THE TOUCH, THE EDGE LIES JUST BEYOND THE ASPEN GROVES, PAST THE SHADED, DAMP PLACES WHERE alluringly red and poisonous mushrooms poke through the leaf litter. The edge spans the horizon, leaving no way for someone to walk around it. Beyond it, the Grand Canyon unfolds.

Ravens sail over the threshold, circling above canyons that unravel 5,600 feet below their wings. I imagine that these birds rejoice over their action, that they fly in ecstasy. I am held to the ground while the ravens in front of me trace shapes in the sky at my eye level.

The rim here consists of catwalks, platforms, and arches. I walk out on one of these tapered slabs of rock, getting as close as I can to the ravens. The landscape beneath me looks like a shifting skeleton of the planet, rich with many shapes. A first impression might suggest that the shapes are haphazard, a drunken scattering of cliffs and canyons. But another few minutes of watching reveals a system.

Stacks of rock colors repeat themselves at intervals. A cliff, identified by certain contours, flows in and out of canyons, like a person running fingers along a tangled ribbon to find its ends. This kind of land implies that more is hidden down there than a person could uncover in a lifetime.

There is no particular way to witness the Grand Canyon. If you see it from the Rim, the place is laid open. It casts a noble view, showing clearly that the Grand Canyon embodies much more than canyons; it is a vastness.

But you cannot see the Canyon's finer details and innuendoes from this far up. Walk down into it, and you will find rims and terraces and sandstone tables stretching for miles. At the bottom, you will step by seashell fossils on the desert floor, ancient life turned into stone in perfect form. Spend days in one branch of a side canyon — sleeping in its sandstone hollows, drinking floodwater, studying the movements of canyon wrens and the delicately curved spines on a fishhook cactus. Then walk back to the highest rim and look over the handprint of canyons behind you. You will have an inkling of knowledge about the Grand Canyon, a handful of notes. But mostly you will be impressed with a raw sense of magnitude.

I am leaving in a few days to begin four months of travel in the Grand Canyon.

At some points I will be joined by companions. After that trek, I will return for smaller ventures into places missed. This will be done on foot mostly. I'll resupply from caches along the way as I follow summer to fall, fall to winter, and winter to spring.

The purpose is not to cover the length of the Canyon, to walk each of its major side canyons, nor to set records. It is to walk the land, focusing on some of its more exquisite, remote details. My intention with the book that comes out of this is to describe what cannot be revealed through photographs, while Gary Ladd is out there, somewhere, photographing what cannot be revealed in words.

I came to this point today to gaze across the Canyon before starting my journey.

A thunderstorm makes its way over the South Rim and then along the Colorado River like a fingertip of God tracing a line a hundred miles across the landscape. The progress of one of these storms requires half a day to watch. Thunder comes, embedding sound — booms and cracks — into the deepest canyons. So much looms here, so many dark turns and towering walls, that it is difficult to look straight into it. With my boot, I clear away some small rocks. I crouch on a slab of white limestone, then lie on my side, curling against the parent rock as the rain begins. I close my eyes to sleep through the afternoon.

Opposite: From the North Rim's Cape Royal, an August sun pours through the clouds to silhouette distant Zoroaster Temple.

INTRODUCTION

GARY LADD

HERE'S THE PARADOX: ONE OF THE GREAT JOYS OF THE GRAND CANYON IS THAT YOU CAN STEP TO THE FOREST'S EDGE AT AN OVERLOOK AND SEEMINGLY SEE IT ALL — TEMPLES, BUTTES, inner gorge, river, rock strata — all exhibited in exquisite three-dimension. Yet, it also is true that from the Rim you have seen nothing.

Below the Rim, another world unfolds. Down there, inside, standing at the edge of the Colorado River, the rim world is as remote as another continent. On the Rim, you are a detached observer; by the river, you are a participant.

The Canyon's orderly arrangement is astonishing: the rim of Kaibab limestone; the imposing escarpments of the Redwall; the arrangement of boulders, pebbles, and sand in a bone-dry streambed; the mesquite trees gathered on the benches; the architecture of the alcoves; the conchoidal curves of the Supai sandstones; and the Esplanade, Tonto platform, Tapeats ledges, and Muav steps.

The Grand Canyon possesses a coherence like no other landscape I know. Its predictable characteristics make the Grand Canyon a steadfast friend to those who grow to know it — a friend whose distinctive features will be recognized instantly from Lees Ferry to Grand Wash Cliffs. Yet no matter how well someone thinks he knows it, the Canyon forever springs surprises, clever variations just slightly out of character.

The Grand Canyon has more than coherence. It possesses power: power in its rapids, in its size, in its cliffs, and in its portrayal of time.

The Grand Canyon is a powerful physical structure analogous to a great mansion. You can view it from the outside and appreciate its architecture. But only from the inside, below the Rim, can you fully appreciate the Grand Canyon. It's a labyrinth. Within it lie tens of thousands of corridors, rotundas, secret staircases, dungeons, ballrooms, staterooms, boudoirs, chambers, arboretums, parlors, attics, and libraries. Side canyons branch into sub-canyons that divide into channels that lead to ravines that develop on the surfaces of plateaus that lie far below the Rim. No one will ever know it all. No one.

Down at the bottom, often hidden in a dark and gloomy trench of crystalline rock, rumbles the Colorado River, the Canyon's supreme thread of potency and enchantment, and its power's ultimate expression.

Butterflies still flutter through my midsection when I approach the brink of a Grand Canyon trailhead. My familiarity with the Grand Canyon's predictable coherence, gained from many hundreds of days spent along and below its rims, is not enough to completely assuage my trepidation when confronted with its authority.

Power and coherence. Can such a place possibly be adequately photographed? I don't think so. Photographs can portray shards of the sublimity of the place. But photographs have little success depicting power and coherence. That can be recorded only in the mind and accomplished only by descending the Grand Canyon's trails, shooting its rapids, and sitting quietly in a chamber hewn from rock hundreds of millions of years old.

Opposite: Downstream from Sockdologer Rapids, in the depths of Upper Granite Gorge, the Colorado River surges with urgency.

Following panel: A February sunrise illuminates Badger Rapids, the first of the Grand Canyon's cataracts.

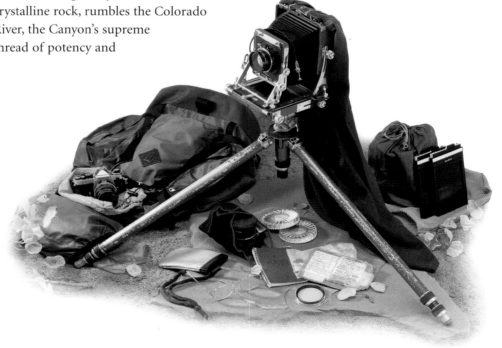

THE LONG, DEEP TRAILS OF WATER

A WAVE SPREADS IN FRONT OF MY CHEST, FANNING AWAY AND TAPPING THE CANYON WALLS BEFORE PURLING BACK. I HOLD MY PACK over my head to keep it out of the water. I stop and listen. Silence. The canyon swallows the sounds my partner makes downstream. Ahead, the Redwall limestone curves. It curves again in the opposite direction. Then comes another curve as the canyon slices through solid stone. Its walls are fluted and deeply scalloped by floods.

WATER, THE BLADE THAT CUT EACH OF THESE CANYONS, RANKS AS THE ELEMENT OF CONSEQUENCE HERE. WATER LAID THESE CANYONS TO THEIR DEPTHS. IT HAS GIVEN THE GRAND CANYON ITS UNMISTAKABLE BREADTH.

You don't come in here by mistake. The inner passageways of these canyons curve too steeply, lie too remote for you to just stumble across them. Here, you shiver with isolation. In this place, you spread your hands against rock and breathe. Satellites and airplanes could never spot you. All this constitutes a quality of wilderness drawing you to the interior of the Grand Canyon, a place draped into a web of a thousand canyons.

The name Grand Canyon implies that the abyss consists of only one canyon, a giant crack in the landscape of northern Arizona. Actually, there are more than 600 canyons here, most of them dry, some harboring small perennial streams.

These canyons are tributaries of the Colorado River. Perforating the curve of

Opposite: Standing across from the mouth of Havasu Canyon near SB Point in the western Grand Canyon, an observant visitor can identify the endless intricacies of the Esplanade — the flat terrain covering much of the photo — and Mount Sinyala. The Colorado River (not visible) flows in the Canyon below the visitor.

local plateaus, they fan out like wings from a 280-mile stretch of river, breaking into feathers, then into vanes and tines. Tributaries split in half and split, and split again. Counting branch by branch, the canyons eventually number in the thousands. Few of the canyons have names. Fewer have trails. In most, decades will pass between human footprints.

The canyon I'm in widens and tightens as if breathing. Overhead, ellipsoidal bulges of limestone block the sky. Several weeks ago, I watched a flash flood cascade from the rims and enter this canyon, sending a dun-colored mist straight up the walls. The floodwater remains. It seeps cold and clear from springs, spilling through consecutive pools. Some places are filled chin-deep, while others are left only with swollen, damp sand at the bottom. Boulders, some of them a fine-grained sandstone from four miles away, are lodged in and above the water, carried here by the flood. Where passing boulders have struck the walls, the limestone has turned a powdery white. Above that, a steel gray defines the canyon, and farther up — 300 feet over my head — the stone has absorbed a red stain from the leaking iron oxide of formations 4,000 feet above. The deepness of the canyon and the absorptive color of the walls works the afternoon light into a dimness no stronger than a gibbous moon. I tip my head in the half-light and drink from the canyon floor. No need to carry water.

People call this canyon SB, rumored to be a shortened version of SOB. People who once corralled cattle along one of the rims used the term to describe the effort it took to get around in this terrain.

SB lies on the north side of the Colorado River, in the center of Grand Canyon National Park. To get this far, we have used almost every piece of climbing equipment we brought. We've built ladders of webbing over boulders and clipped rope into firm anchors. Days have been spent seeking routes and returning to camp, climbing narrow cracks in waterfalls.

When I come around a turn, finally climbing from the water and seating my pack over my shoulders, I find my partner. He stands straining to see down from the tip of a boulder. He looks back at me. The way he smiles, I know we have come to another dead end. The boulder, seven feet wide, has wedged into the canyon floor, creating a talkative waterfall below.

We will have to climb. Again.

WATER, THE BLADE THAT CUT each of these canyons, ranks as the element of consequence here. There is, of course, the slow crafting of wind and

gravity, the exfoliating collapse of cliff faces over time, the tug of tectonics. But water laid these canyons to their depths. It has given the Grand Canyon its unmistakable breadth.

On first glance, it might seem that something the size of the Colorado River cut each canyon. The highest rims may be miles apart, the bottoms so precisely inset, that you might imagine great Ice Age rivers carving their way to the bottom of the continent. But walk to the floor of each canyon, and you will find a narrow wash or carved bedrock showing where a stream once flowed. The bed likely will be dry.

That streams so small and rare could cut canyons of this size makes little sense. The time frame for this kind of erosion may seem staggering. But don't be fooled. Water that moves over stone is staggeringly influential.

Customarily, the water comes as floods. The canyons formed from a

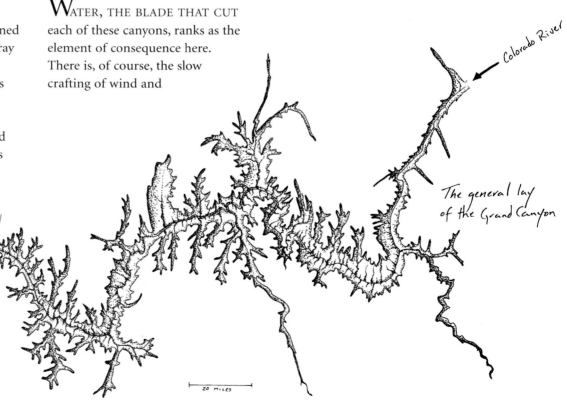

Colorado River

The general lay of the Grand Canyon

Grand Wash Cliffs

20 miles

litany of flash floods over millions of years, not by a few catastrophic floods. Rarely do floods last more than several hours. Sometimes, they last only 20 or 30 minutes. They follow the whims of isolated storms, coming to a particular location a couple of times in one year or only once a decade. They form in distant tributaries and gain force through the deepening hallways of inner gorges, aiming for the lowest common denominator — the Colorado River. The river, sunk into the Kaibab Plateau, forms a base level to which all surrounding water must travel. Floods have marked their passages to the river, leaving the land a scarred complexion.

The flood I witnessed here weeks ago threw boulders and trees down the throats of canyons. Relentlessly, the water drove deep into the canyon like columns of pounding cavalry horses. During three hours of rising and falling, the flood utterly rearranged the floors of several canyons, dropping boulders miles from their previous locations. The place filled with violence, with an industrial howling of mud, water, and stone. Then, as the beds drained and dried, absolute silence descended.

This was one of the million brief etchings that, like a single word added to the rest, combine eventually to tell the story. When you look into these canyons, keep this in mind: Water has crafted what you see.

In lab experiments with running water and a resistant, concrete-like substance, lowering the base level constitutes the only way to cut a good channel. This means lowering the elevation of the water's destination. For

side canyons of the Grand Canyon, the Colorado River serves as the base level. For the Colorado River, it is the Sea of Cortes. The lowering of the base level puts more vertical distance between the top and bottom of a drainage, and the water pierces the ground in search of equilibrium. The further these lab streams are stretched from their base levels, the more they form channels resembling miniature portions of the Grand Canyon.

You can lower the base level or raise the land with the same results. For about 10 million years, the Kaibab Plateau and a number of neighboring humps of land have been rising out of the earth like whales, and across their backs flows the Colorado River. As land rose, the river dug harder into the continent to lower itself to base level. The river, having a far more constant flow than its mostly dry tributaries, cut quickly toward equilibrium, leaving hundreds of tributaries teetering at the edge of a deepening gorge. With their base level pulled out from under them, these smaller canyons have struggled to catch up. They have disemboweled themselves at every occasion of flash floods, trying to flatten their gradients to the river.

These forces shaped the Grand Canyon. The Colorado River alone would have carved one 200-foot-wide chasm and left it at that. But water began trickling down from storms and streams on all sides. In their attempt to equalize with the river, 600 struggling tributaries have spread through the desert countryside until canyon space exceeds land. They are still working. If you want to see the true nature of animated, dynamic geology in the Grand Canyon, look into the side canyons. Staying awake for a night in a canyon, you may hear boulders and smaller

rocks tapping and crashing as they fall. The action comes in the distant, unlit places where the landscape will not rest.

I CAME HERE IN AUGUST TO TRAVEL for weeks across red benches of Esplanade sandstone looming over lower levels of canyons. Every 10 days or so on this solo walk, I reached a food cache where I would linger for a night, restocking my pack with chocolate, rice, and potato flakes. Nights were brief and clouded with stars. Days were long and well over 100° F. I spent my afternoons in shade, creeping from one boulder to the next, curling against the cool rock when I stopped, like an animal accustomed to sleeping on the ground. Cliff faces baked in sunlight, heating the surrounding air. I shaved my head. I did not carry a sleeping bag and often slept naked among the rocks, covering myself with a cotton sheet if a breeze picked up.

The Park Service had asked me to write a report on a trail that was supposed to cross this region. After 20 days, I found only a few cairns and narrow clearings 30 or 40 feet long that might have been remnants of a trail. I would return with my report: There is no trail, only a route.

I reached the top of SB Canyon in September, seeking refuge in its inner shadows. Down into the canyon at dawn, my gear left tucked into the rocks for safekeeping, I followed the deep bucket-like depressions that floods had carved from bedrock. The air, moist before sunrise, smelled strongly of something like freshly cut herbs. Cottonwood and western redbud trees, monkeyflower, and seepwillow shrubs. I stopped for a while to listen to a spring. A drop of water fell every 15 or 30

The Fury and Artistry of Flash Floods

Above Left: A bloody stream surges toward a meeting with the Colorado River in Conquistador Aisle at River Mile 122 — 122 miles downstream from Lees Ferry — in late July.

Above: Laden with silt from the Moenkopi formation, Soap Creek acquires the viscosity of machine oil during an October flood.

Left: Near River Mile 155, where Paradise Canyon joins the Colorado River, the pool basin bears a rusty color painted by summer floods.

seconds, tapping the surface of a pool I could not see. The sound was so private that when I stood and walked ahead, I did not look back to find it.

Deeper into the canyon, formations arose around me. When a light blue bed of limestone appeared beneath my feet, the canyon plunged. Now, set within it, a line ran straight into the canyon floor. It was another canyon, dark as a cave even as the sun came up. I walked the edge, looking down. The passage 50 feet below did not look accessible. As far as I could see, it deepened. One hundred feet, 200 feet, and tight as a church aisle. I climbed in where I could, taking handholds in the limestone until my boots touched the canyon floor. Polished, flood-burrowed limestone rounded into a small creek. I swam in the deeper stretch where water had pooled. Maidenhair ferns crowded at small waterfall springs, the kind frequently exposed in the Redwall limestone. My presence set into motion a clockwork of pools below. Matching exactly the volume of my body, water spun down a chute, topping the next reservoir, and spilling over again. The repercussions of my act sent word into the canyon.

I could go only so far. A boulder choked the narrow passage, and, for me, SB stopped. I crawled onto the boulder's back and looked over. I didn't even try to go farther. My body would never be found if I made a mistake. I sat, staring as far as I could see. As it left my view, falling water casually conversed with its own echoes, pure as love and unattainable. The longer I sat and listened, the more I felt that I was rubbing shoulders with more mystery than I could bear. Desire to go on

enveloped me strongly, but everything was out of reach.

Two days later, I walked to a rim several hundred feet above this place. Still a thousand feet below the highest rim, I was somewhere in the middle, walking the broad shelf of Esplanade sandstone. I drank from water holes in the open desert — whatever water I could find, brushing away layers of insect bodies before touching my lips to the surface. The water would be gone in a day or two. Monstrous stone temples stretched back for miles. Over SB Canyon, a raven soared, making fascinating designs in the sky. It grumbled and spoke sharply to me. One feather was out of place, or was stripped, because each time the raven swung back, catching the air just so, its feather whined like a mosquito. I followed the sound to the edge.

From there, I looked into SB, miles down to the narrow crack that had stopped me days earlier. Now it looked like a paper cut in the limestone. The bottom was nowhere in sight. If this were anywhere else, it would be a monument, a place to come and stare at the terrifying power of nature. A metal railing would prevent fascination from taunting you right off the edge.

An Arizona sister butterfly found on the canyon floor.

The fact that I could not get inside forced me to look away, to scheme, to give up and look back in. The raven came so close on its next pass that when I lifted my hand to block the sun, the bird veered away in surprise.

THE NEXT TIME I LEFT THE Canyon, I reached a pay phone in Kanab, Utah, and called Tom Vimont. We had worked as guides and instructors for years on the Colorado River, taking our days between trips to wander into the deserts of southern Arizona. He had once taught mountaineering. He knows how to use ropes, how to get into unattainable locations.

I told him about this snip of a canyon that would turn his world inside out. Instead of climbing up a mountain, we would climb down a canyon. We would go until the sky closed over our heads. I called him at work, told him to meet me at the end of a 60-mile dirt road, and hung up before he could say no.

Broad-shouldered and bulky, Tom likes to bleed, and laugh as the blood flows. I've emptied first-aid kits on him after scrambling through cracks and loose rock. Talking to him is like having confetti thrown in your face. His voice is loud, his words pointed. He does not fear what people think. I sat with him once in the desert and, after a long time of saying nothing, he looked over to me.

"You know, I wouldn't mind being a cave man," he said. "Eating and hunting and having sex and sleeping. That is a good life."

At various times, he worked as a three-star chef in Chicago, an exotic dancer in some other city, a climbing instructor for Outward Bound, and a singer for a punk rock band. Our histories have little similarity. This allows us to travel well together. He seems to be afraid of nothing. But even coming with a partner, I feel a solitary fascination from the days I stared down off the rim. We only need each other to stay alive. This is how we often have traveled together, sprawling beneath stars at camp after difficult days and telling our stories back to each other.

He has bread maker's hands, his fingers strong and meaty on a rope. At the boulder that has stopped us, he unravels some webbing and ties loops into it. Even if we pass this point, we do not know if we can find a way down. Only one piece of webbing remains in our gear, and so far each piece of equipment has been necessary. Tom shrugs at the possibilities and sets the webbing.

This thin lifeline dangles down the crack between the boulder and the wall. I enter first. My strength quickly wanes as I tip backwards, shifting various small muscles to hold my body in place. The space is not quite large enough. My chest jams between boulder and wall, and I exhale to squeeze myself further. The boulder has been wedged so long that it has been carved by floods. I groan and reach down, dropping notch by notch, the walls slick and not taking to my fingers.

I lower myself into a pool and wade across to watch Tom work his way down. We intend to reach the Colorado River, then climb back along these same routes. But the river may as well not exist. There is nothing but this canyon. I feel as if I must hold my breath as I walk through. The walls swing from side to side, forming overlapping waves that look more like water than rock. There is no true floor, only a depression of water and gravel or a curve of scoured bedrock. The limestone exhibits structural soundness, especially when compared to the higher slopes of Hermit shale or the cliffs of Coconino sandstone; it will not cave in as it is incised. It braces into position, allowing this canyon to wind deeply. As it resists floods, the limestone takes peculiar shapes. Walls turn smooth like bone, as intricate as vertebrae or the ball of a femur.

Someone once asked if I grow bored with canyons, if the repetition of drainages wears on me after months. I could not find words to explain. I merely said no. To express an eternal fascination with them would peg me as a starry-eyed naturalist loping merrily from canyon to canyon. But each canyon inscribes a signature so descriptive that it is difficult to talk about more than one

Maidenhair fern, Adiantum capillus-veneris

at a time. I will be very clear about this. The canyons are only similar in that they often involve rock and cliffs and some sign of water. That is all.

The unnamed canyon west of Garnet Canyon turns into a tight sliver before a 700-foot fall into bands of Bright Angel shale. Haunted Canyon levels into a remote grove of cottonwood trees, the floor flickering with shadows. A tributary to an arm of Tuckup Canyon has a scoop that could seat a symphony orchestra but instead holds five strands of maidenhair fern, each releasing small slips of spring water. Various portions of the Grand Canyon between Lees Ferry and Pearce Ferry have vastly different terrain. Side canyons with mouths facing each other at the river — one on the north, the other south — bear, in their interiors, distinctions as pronounced as differences between a midnight sky and a sunrise.

Compared to the variety of side canyons, the river's canyon ranks as elementary. The Colorado River often burrows straight through structural, geomorphic controls such as faults and regional dips in the strata. The river gives little preference to what it erodes. But side canyons, with less stream force, must contend with the slighter nuances of geology. Side canyons are engrossed in pivoting and pushing through formations, creating intricate profiles that alter over the thousands and millions of years.

The Grand Canyon stretches across a plateau that dips steadily south. Its highest rim is the North Rim — more than 1,000 feet higher than the South Rim. North Rim canyons flow down the dip and linger beneath long ridges. South Rim canyons, which must work against the grain of the dip, plunge off the Rim, hitting the river quickly.

Sculptured Chambers and Sinuous Corridors

Above: Smooth contours of Muav limestone set a tone of graceful simplicity near the mouth of Matkatamiba Canyon.

Above Right: A frog chooses to ignore the intrusive behavior of large mammals.

Right: Hikers find a refuge from the rising heat in Silver Grotto near River Mile 29.

The eastern portion of the South Rim near Desert View has few canyons because of low rainfall, low runoff, and rock layers leaning away from the river. A little west, as you walk along Comanche Point and its surrounding saddles, canyons will open under your feet and plunge directly to the river. Slightly farther west, weak shales are exposed, allowing numerous broad canyons to form. And even farther west, deeper, narrow canyons drill through newly exposed Vishnu schist that lies solidly in the floor.

Most of the canyons falling off the South Rim are dry or hold only small ephemeral creeks. The canyons are simple, rarely branching more than once or twice.

Meanwhile, across the river, rainfall and snowmelt off the extensive North Rim feed long and crowded canyon systems. Their branches flow radially down the curved southern and western flanks of the Kaibab Plateau.

Interestingly, floods from the curt and declivitous South Rim canyons produce larger, more rocky debris than do the wetter, longer North Rim canyons, suggesting that the steepness on the south side sustains higher levels of erosion.

There are influences that will turn a canyon into a sine wave, causing it to hollow out amphitheaters, or giving it a gentle, stair-step descent. But the highest authority on canyon-forming stems from geologic faulting. The entire underside of the Grand Canyon is loaded with faults. Most of these cracks in solid, underlying rock trend northeast with a few skirting at odd angles. The slipping of the faults has left impressive forms and many colorful names: Crazy Jug Monocline, Dragon Fault, Blue Moon Graben, Eminence Fault.

There are formations of substantial length, such as the Kaibab Monocline, which runs more than 150 miles from a point near Flagstaff to Utah. It has 5,000 feet of displacement — that is, one side is 5,000 feet higher than the other. But displacement of others — less than half a mile long — may be only the width of a finger. I have traced massive rockfalls to faults, walked behind the tilted back of a collapsed 200-foot block and found there an exposed axis of a fault.

Looking at a surface geology map of the Grand Canyon, you will see that nearly every side canyon, and even minor tributaries, follow faults, most of which predate the Canyon by millions, if not billions, of years. Unrelated canyons can be lined up with a ruler because underneath, like an underground passageway, lies a connecting fault. Like interlocked fingers, a side canyon of Unkar Creek points directly into the head of Asbestos Canyon. The upper arms of Vishnu Creek are parallel with each other and with the canyon on the opposite side of Krishna Shrine. Walking up Stairway Canyon near Toroweap, you can stop halfway and turn to see the slot of Mohawk Canyon on the opposite side of the river, both canyons aligned over a straight fault that crosses the river. Nearly every small canyon has a trailing twin nearby. This is not routine behavior for canyons cutting with

various forces into differing rock. It implies that below is a key to the entire layout of the Grand Canyon.

If a canyon severs a fault, rocks on either side of the fault are weakened and collapse. So, as floods spill into a fault, they cut downward, rending the fault's support. The walls then fail, and floods carry the debris out. Debris adds abrasiveness to the floods. Thus, they cut deeper into the faults, severing them again and opening the canyons even further.

That phenomenon compares to a roadway being cut into a steep side of a valley. Construction likely will sever a fault, causing landslides to repeatedly blanket the road, leaving engineers cursing and wondering why nature plagues them so.

Upstream in the Grand Canyon, Marble Canyon follows the southwest-trending grain of local faulting. Few faults run perpendicular to the river along this upper stretch, so there is little interference with the river canyon, leaving fewer side canyons. The river then takes an unprecedented swing to the west. It lays faults open to the sky, and side canyons grow into the fissures like splintering glass.

I once hiked with a geologist to this point where the river jumped its

Western redbud branch,
Cercis occidentalis

tracks. We set camp on the Colorado Lineament, an ancient and deep basement structure that runs from here to Wyoming and keeps the river in its course nearly back to the Colorado border. The area, down Tanner Canyon, is a mess. We saw growth faults, thrust faults, reverse faults, anticlines, monoclines, synclines, folds, warps, slump blocks, unconformities, and chevron folds in twisted solid rock. Looking north, we could see up the line of Marble Canyon. West showed where the river turns out of the Colorado Lineament and rattles over a washboard of faults all the way to Nevada.

The river should continue south to Phoenix, but instead, it takes this heroic run the other way across the Kaibab Plateau, opening the stage for hundreds of side canyons to pour into the newly exposed faults.

This geologist stood looking straight up the Colorado Lineament, into Marble Canyon, grinning as if he were standing on the line where the continent soon would split in two. He said it might some day. The lineament is part of longer, deeper systems that extend to Canada. Sometimes it is wide enough to occupy an entire mountain range and here creates swarming fault systems to feed the Grand Canyon.

In a way, the Grand Canyon was formed because the river resisted the grain of the lineament and took a dive to the west. This turn, where the inner gorge rebounds off Palisades of the Desert and Tanner Canyon, sent the river into a nest of faults and fractures. The underside of this landscape must look like a spider web. Across its surface, canyons fall into place like insects caught on strands, outlining the invisible web below.

This is why I cannot tire of these canyons.

I WALK DEEPER AND THE HALF-light turns to quarter-light. Few signs of life show themselves down here: a tree frog, pale and still as a river cobble; several desert rock nettles grown from cracks well out of the flood zone, hanging 30 feet off the floor; a dragonfly after prey with the grace and quickness of a cutting horse.

I come to the next obstacle, another array of rocks jammed between two walls. One of these chockstones lies low on the floor, building waterfalls through its seams. Another is left suspended where a flood once jammed it between walls. This second boulder, four feet high, hangs 30 feet off the floor. The arrangement looks as if it were hand-placed by someone with a sense of order and artistry.

Below is a pool. Bottomless, as far as I can see. The curve of the route is difficult, the length of the drop daunting. Tom stands beside me and we look down, hoping to see a handhold or some small crack that can aid in getting us up and down. There is nothing to say. The final piece of webbing is brought out. Loops tied. Anchored and lowered into place. It does not reach the water. We will have to go to the end, then drop. Coming back, we'll have to swim under it and reach, in hopes of snatching the line. Sounds impossible.

For 10 minutes we look into this water. A 40-ton boulder hangs before our heads. "I'll be the scapegoat," Tom finally says. "I don't think I can do this." I study his eyes. I don't think I can do it, either. The canyon has ended.

Tom has ideas about how to get to the end of this canyon. They involve some other time, coming in with a

certain amount of rope, pulling it down behind us to use on the boulders ahead, finding a route out from the river, perhaps up Kanab Creek or Tuckup Canyon. Staring into the water, he unravels his plans. He asks me what month would be good and, man, it would have been something to have reached the river, wouldn't it?

I am looking into the same water. The canyon still is not mine. Never will be mine. The satisfaction of this is rich and inexplicable. With understandable reluctance, Tom reels the webbing back up the rock. It catches a couple times between boulder and wall, and he snaps it loose. When the last few feet are slithered up, he unclips the carabiner, and the canyon beyond falls from my grasp. It is dusky and curved, drawing water into subterranean shapes just out of view, down where the stream echoes around boulders. The enigma down there is raw. It is a clear and perfect reminder of what is out here, what the land is made of. Secrets are everywhere, and meant to be kept.

At night we set a meager camp on stream cobbles a quarter-mile upstream. We listen to the ornate, etching sounds of water over small rocks. Above us, a series of escape ledges provide space where we can scramble if a flood should come down the canyon.

But we give little thought to floods tonight. Just thoughts of this canyon. We do not have sleeping bags or pads. Only sand and delicately rounded stones. We each find a place to sleep. Tucking hands under my head, I curl into the rocks, again like an animal. Stars gather in the narrow cleft of sky, and I swear that if I reach up, they will spill, powdering my face.

MODEST BEGINNINGS

THE GRAND CANYON DOES NOT BEGIN GRANDLY.
IN FACT, A TANGLE OF ESCARPMENTS AND GORGES CAMOUFLAGE ITS BIRTH,
making it an understated beginning.

At Lees Ferry, Arizona, Glen Canyon abruptly ends at a bend in the Colorado River. Cliffs veer off in all directions — south for the Echo Cliffs, southwest for the Vermilion Cliffs, and northwest for the walls of Paria Canyon. Downstream along the Colorado River, lost amid all this soaring terrain, the Kaibab limestone angles up out of the water. Pass by this subtle ledge of creamy-colored rock and you have entered the portals to Grand Canyon. Only at Lees Ferry do the river and the rim of the Grand Canyon lie at the same elevation, 3,100 feet.

The orange sandstones of Glen and Paria canyons fall back and give way to the new regime. For nearly a hundred miles, the rims of the Grand Canyon inconspicuously will rise into the sky while the river rasps down into the earth.

It is a subtle but wonderfully effective development. For a person floating down the river in a boat or raft, each of the Canyon's rock layers is introduced at river level. Each layer takes its turn as river escort, then politely gives way as another stratam, one still deeper, still older, emerges. Limestones polish up to a marble gloss; red sandstone blocks cantilever out over the restless river; shales erode easily into slopes that counterpoint the cliffs. The boulders derived from bedrock spill out into the river to form noisy rapids with astonishing collections of earth-pieces transported by floods. Side canyons gradually develop as the rims soar higher — first as playful quiet corridors, then, with each passing mile from Lees Ferry, into grand canyons in their own right.

Marble Canyon is a visual symphony. The opus begins simply with a lone instrument, Kaibab limestone. Building on this, the theme of creation is elaborated as new sandstone, shale, or limestone layers emerge. The composition swells in complexity and grandeur with each passing mile.

Opposite: Lit by a July sunrise, the Colorado River leaves the Vermilion Cliffs behind as it carves through Kaibab limestone, and the Grand Canyon begins to take shape at Lees Ferry.

Rising Walls, Churning Rapids

Opposite: The rim of Marble Canyon, looming more than 2,000 feet above the Colorado River at River Mile 23, catches first light.

Above: North Canyon Rapids cascades through a tangle of boulders at shore's edge near River Mile 20.

Right: An angular slab of Supai sandstone tilts into the river where the Colorado River drops 10 feet in House Rock Rapids.

Deposited by Nature

Above: A heap of boulders lies at the foot of a rock funnel at the edge of the Colorado at River Mile 26.

Right: A sandstone boulder lies broken where a raging side-canyon flood left it just short of the river in the area of Marble Canyon known as the redwall gorge.

Opposite: In Bert's Canyon, fallen limestone boulders lie strewn below the cliffs.

Ripple Marks and Currents

Following Panel: Fluctuations in the flow of the Colorado River, now regulated by Glen Canyon Dam, alternately sculpt and wash out ripple marks on sandbars, this one at River Mile 49.

Saddle Canyon

Opposite: In the narrows near River Mile 47, a tranquil pool reflects the sunlit cliffs above.

Left: An agave blooming in early June topples from its own weight.

Below: Redbuds reach for a share of the morning light.

Right: On the Nankoweap Delta, the skeletons
Nankoweap of dead mesquite trees divide sunset light on the Rim. Nankoweap is a Paiute word meaning "singing" or "echo canyon."

Below: Cobble stones form a bar and split the current just downstream from Nankoweap Canyon, which joins the Colorado River near River Mile 52.

Opposite: Anasazi people built granaries overlooking the river at Nankoweap. They occupied some 1,000 sites in the Canyon.

Following Panel: The view upstream from
Kwagunt Rapids Kwagunt Rapids, River Mile 56.

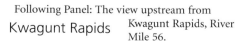

Kwagunt and Malgosa Canyons

Above: Side canyon floods leave a sandbar and pool stained ochre at the edge of the Colorado River just below the mouth of Kwagunt Canyon.

Opposite: An August storm brews over Cape Solitude, while at Malgosa Canyon a limestone boulder's sculpted surface echoes the fan-shaped cloud.

Above: Water sedge thrives along the shore at River Mile 58.

Awatubi Canyon

Left: Late afternoon sun highlights the Facade of the Desert.

A PLACE
FOR
CEREMONY

EXHAUSTED FROM THREE WEEKS OF BACKPACKING, I FIND A LEDGE AND
FOLLOW IT AROUND THE PERIMETER OF A CANYON. MY SHOULDERS
slouch. I have been diving into canyons,
coming out the other side, diving again.
Rather than making linear distance, I
have traveled in tight circles, following
geographic patterns that form links
from a canyon to a rim, back to a
canyon, to a rim . . .

Stalks of thunderstorms
stand against the horizon,
coiling from behind the
canyon rim. These are the
last of the season's
thunderstorms, remnants
of summer mixing with
autumn. Soon, they will be
replaced by the frontal
weather systems of winter,
storms that seem inarticulate
and ponderous compared to
these heat-driven thunderheads.
Fifty miles separate me from
these storms. I do not watch
them out of concern, only out of
curiosity.

I look for an overhang to sleep
beneath. I shuffle into a curved "room,"
scan the ground, and find smooth
sandstone as flat as my back, a good
place to set camp. A slickness to the rock
seems out of place. This kind of sheen
lingers at places where many people
have been, palming the oils of their
hands on the places where they climb or
sit. Archaeological sites, places where

THE HEAD
ARCHAEOLOGIST FOR
GRAND CANYON
NATIONAL PARK
BROUGHT A
VIDEO CAMERA
TO THIS SITE.
EVERY TIME SHE TURNED
THE CAMERA ON,
A STRONG WIND
PICKED UP.
WHEN SHE TURNED
IT OFF, THE
WIND CEASED.

Opposite: A hiker pauses on the South Kaibab Trail near Mather Point, looking over a
landscape that holds the evidence of cultures thousands of years old.

people have spent time for hundreds or thousands of years, bear this sheen. I scan the ground, looking for a sign that people have been here. Eventually, I look up. A small sound escapes my mouth. The walls and ceiling are awash with paintings. I am ashamed I didn't see them earlier, that I was staring at the ground.

These don't come from the Anasazi. I know this immediately. Now and then I find remnants of the Anasazi's stay here: a fist-sized, unfired clay figurine seated in a crack in a canyon east of here, yellow paint drizzled across its body; potsherds tiling the floor of a nearby wash; 900 ochre thumbprints on a smooth rock.

An established desert culture believed to have colonized the Canyon between A.D. 800 and 1050, the Anasazi dabbled in rock art, of course, carving bighorn sheep and curious human-like figures into the heavily varnished cliff faces. These paintings overhead are different. The style makes that clear immediately. It makes the Anasazi artwork seem ridiculously simple, like stick figures. These crowded, intricately rendered figures are the work of people much older than the Anasazi.

There are so many. Hidden within embedded figures are others, and inside of them, still more. Painted green, white, pink, yellow, red, blue. A few animal forms I recognize — deer and bighorn sheep. The remainder, figures four and five feet tall, are not animals. Not humans, either. Some have eyes, maybe. Some have hands. Eighteen large figures are crowded into one segment of a panel. Some have

labyrinthine torsos, painted tightly with different colors. Paint on paint on paint. Shoulder to shoulder. A couple are overlapped to show that one figure is slightly behind another. Seeing this reminds me of hearing a sacred chant in another language — the only thing I know is that the chant embodies tradition and personal sacrifice.

Unlike the more recent Anasazi, no tradition remains from these people to help us glean some idea of the meaning of their artwork. No one knows who they were, or who they might have become. No contemporary tribe has claimed ancestry.

I look outside, at the canyons beyond. Cliffs, boulders, sky. There is no reason this scene should be here. Craning my neck to look straight above, I think, "It is not possible. How have I come here?"

I walk slowly, mindful that my steps do not make a loud sound, that I do not shove one of the small stones sideways, that I do not leave a footprint in sand. I meet their faces over my head. Or what might be faces. Many of the painted lines are thinner than the print on this paper. Brushed with what? A yucca strand? An eyelash? Other lines are as thick as my thumb.

Split-twig figurine from the Grand Canyon.

The style seems similar to the rare Barrier Canyon Style, named after an area in Utah where one of the largest known Archaic-culture panels can be found. Both used similar painting sites, in rock shelters and under overhangs. Both arranged elongated figures in rows across back walls. On these panels, artists paid attention to symmetry and arrangement, producing a composition rarely seen in rock art. On this Grand Canyon panel is a green snake painted over one of the anthropomorphic bodies. I have seen the snake before. It was in Utah, the same color, inside of a figure's gaping mouth.

I've walked in Utah looking for this style of artwork. After stashing a canoe on the Colorado River (to be retrieved months later), I've packed along Cataract Canyon toward Glen Canyon. Up there, in the rounded alcoves of Navajo sandstone, a number of these panels revealed themselves, often as solitary panels, dramatic with detail. The Colorado Plateau is speckled with this style, beginning up near the Book Cliffs of Utah and following the Colorado River and Green River drainages to right here, to this panel.

These people are known as the Western Archaics. They were hunter-gatherers and makers of baskets and various woven goods. They carried small tools for digging and atlatls for killing game. Being hunter-gatherers, they had more leisure time than the agriculturists who came later. This may explain the greater depth to their ceremonies and the more imaginative art motifs. As people became more involved in repetitive and labor-intensive agriculture, the smaller and less detailed their rock art figures became.

In color, peculiarity, and size, these hunter-gatherer images loom over

Anasazi work. Exact dating, of course, is difficult. Barrier Canyon sites in Utah have produced radiocarbon dates of about 3,300 years before the present. But unfired clay figurines that mimic these painted figures, and date back nearly 9,000 years, have been discovered.

That the artists exercised great care with this panel stands out. Touch-up work is evident, most certainly done by the Archaics themselves. The outline of one figure was retouched with red and the heads of two others were redone in a dark green. The figures were important enough that as they deteriorated over time, people came to make repairs.

I have talked with the head archaeologist for Grand Canyon National Park about this panel. She once hiked here to document the place, and although she has terse, less-mystical interpretations of a great deal of rock art in the Southwest, this one stops her cold. She said this site seems to be ceremonial. Not just ceremonial, but supernatural. She brought a video camera. Every time she turned the camera on, she said, a strong wind picked up. When she turned it off, the wind ceased. "There is something very different there," she said. For a trained, high-level archaeologist, these are not idle words.

I am thinking that I must tell you of every detail that I witness here. Otherwise, the significance of this panel might be lost. But there is too much to tell. After coming back the next morning and sketching for several hours, I finally see a third layer of figures painted beneath the first and second. There is no way I can convey this. Bodies are divided into sections, with designs entered into their interior compartments. Many of the hands of figures bear red dots in their open palms. An animal, a carnivore of some sort, is painted in green, its tail, claws, ears, and eyes highlighted with red. Photographs and drawings won't do. Even being here to see it would not be enough. The light would be different. You would not be looking for the same elements. I will see eyes where you see geometry. You will see blood thrown against the rock where I see spare dabs of iron oxide pigment.

So I will choose this one, a small painting on a far side of the panel. Of all these impressive, alien forms, the one that strikes me most is this, a painting of a deer. It is 10 inches long. It is a simple rendering, yet there is an astounding attention to detail. In one, maybe two

strokes, the artist prepared an image that comes only from close observation of the animal. The delicate sway of the back. The thickness of thighs in the hind legs. A tail not poked from the rear end, but curved off the base of the spine where it belongs. Hind hooves cloven, spread as they would during a run or while slowly navigating difficult terrain. Antlers, each with the same number of points, bearing short spikes at the base. The throat not tapering until it meets the breast. The thinness of the legs above the hooves.

It appears to have been created in much the same fashion as a Japanese ink painting on silk, where the brush tip is controlled from the shoulder and not from the hand. Whatever brush was used, I believe that it touched the rock and left it in a single stroke. Such candid work must be honest. Whatever skill or knowledge was held by this painter, it is revealed here. While the other paintings leave me boggled, this one suggests something about the artist. The rest are works of wizards.

THERE ARE OTHER STORIES OUT here besides this rock art. What archaeologists have found of this pre-Anasazi desert culture has inspired them to use terms such as magico-religious to refer to rituals and sacred acts, when, in fact, there is hardly enough information to say what these people were wearing. It is just that a sense of ceremony pervades their artifacts.

The other stories come in the form of wooden animal figures, most small enough to fit in your palm. Like the style of painting from this period, these wooden pieces are specific in form, geographically isolated, and rich with ceremonial overtones. Each is made from a willow or squaw bush twig. The

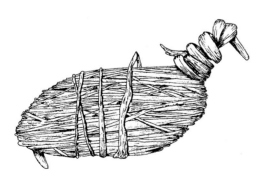

A figurine wrapped in grass with bark around the neck and head, and a figurine with "horns."

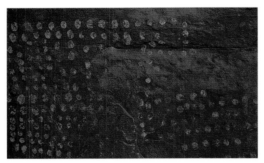

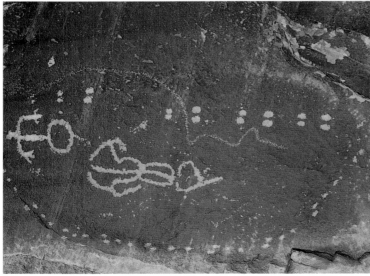

Art and Tools of Ancient People

Above: Rock walls and manos and metates — rocks used to grind grain — mark an Anasazi Indian site in a tributary of Upper Granite Gorge.

From Top Left: Supai sandstone serves as a canvas for pictographs, paintings believed to be several thousands of years old.

Pictographs on the north side of the Colorado River: Could they be a tally of visits? Big horn sheep? Days? Years?

Prehistoric Canyon residents incised these petroglyphs in Coconino sandstone along an ancient trail.

twig is split down the center, but not completely severed. Like folding one paper sheet for origami, the twig is taken through a number of steps. It is wrapped around itself repeatedly at different lengths and angles until a body, legs, neck, and head are formed. A deer — or something like it — from a single, unbroken twig.

The oldest of these date back about 4,000 years. Whether the painters of this rock art and the makers of these wooden figures had anything to do with each other is not clear. Two figurine sites were found in Utah, in the same canyon system where the largest Barrier Canyon rock art panels were found. What is clear from this time period is that whoever they were, these people had explicit styles. They created objects that adhered to rules used across great distances.

Still, there are variations. Some of these split-twig figurines appear to have been made quickly, or without rehearsal. There are those with heads obtrusively large, or those made with twigs too fat to be easily folded. Mostly, however, they are woven tight as baskets, the twigs bent carefully so that every line is flush. A small number of the figurines discovered in the Grand Canyon are pierced with lances of cottonwood or agave, possibly representing a hunting practice. Others might encase the droppings of animals. A pellet from a bighorn sheep or a deer (the difference can be seen in the shape) is placed within the body cavity, as if to relate a certain species to the individual figurine. Horns occasionally are seen, an effect achieved by adding extra wraps with the twig. The horns frequently are cinched to the head with additional material, perhaps a piece of vine. Grass bundles are sometimes used, wrapped around the completed

figurine, tightened with vine or bark. Some archaeologists have suggested that the grass, which completely covers the body and allows only the legs and head to show, represents winter fur.

What is most stirring about these artifacts is where they are found. Always, they are in caves. They are found only in those caves that extend far enough to become completely dark. Some of these require the use of harnesses and ropes across the faces of 600-foot cliffs. But there is no evidence that these people used any sort of climbing apparatus, other than feet and fingers. The caves most difficult to access have produced the greatest number of figurines. One archaeologist explained to me the physical access to one of the caves. He described kissing the wall in order to swing his arm around a blind corner from a ledge. There he felt for a handhold, dug his fingers in, and pulled his body around, suspended for a moment over a 400-foot plummet.

The consensus among archaeologists is that these figurines were strictly ceremonial and that no one ever lived in these caves. The range of radiocarbon dates shows that the figurines were placed over an 830-year period. Countless generations came to these caves, leaving meager but distinct

signs of their presence. The physical, recorded acts were simple: the construction of a small figure and perhaps the rearrangement of rocks already on the floor. The person would have backed away without dropping a stone tool or leaving a shred of basketry. Because these were identical acts, repeated perfectly for eight centuries, they are imbued with great significance. Whatever else was done in these caves, whatever singing or waving of incense, it was done with care and left no clue.

Many hundreds of these figurines from caves in Nevada, Utah, Arizona, and the Grand Canyon have been cataloged. Occasionally, they appear in private collections, such as those recently seen at a trading post in Moab, Utah, and a gallery in Cameron, Arizona. But they are not generic like baskets or sandals. They show patterns as isolated as summer thunderstorms. Hundreds of miles might lie between one site and the next. But even so scattered, three-quarters of the known split-twig figurines in the world have come from the caves of the Grand Canyon region.

The figurines of the Grand Canyon are different from those found elsewhere in the desert. Those of the Grand Canyon caves were thoughtfully placed, usually in a grass-lined pit, buried, sometimes burned, beneath stacked

Pictographs, likely Anasazi, painted in white clay.

rocks or in a crack. And they are made with a somewhat redundant style. The act of piercing the figurines with sticks or inserting animal droppings appears to be unique to the Grand Canyon.

Outside of the Grand Canyon, figurine caves are easy to access and sometimes are little more than deep shelters. In these shelters, the figurines are likely to be unkempt among the familiar items of living: the bone and antler tools, the random clay articles, and hammerstones used for breaking smaller rocks.

Those in the Grand Canyon, found in the company of no other artifacts, appear to be hardly touched, not desecrated by the acts of everyday life.

These figurines began to appear in the Southwest about the time of the Babylonian invention of the abacus. A quick look at this juxtaposition assumes the makers of an abacus were far more advanced than the makers of split-twig figurines. But keep in mind that the first abacus was merely a slab upon which sand was spread. Calculations were traced into the sand. A few thousand years passed before the Chinese elevated the abacus to its better known form of beads strung within a frame. The Babylonians dealt in commerce and the counting of commodities. Archaics dealt in canyons and bighorn sheep, where the addition of numbers may have seemed trivial and irrelevant.

A person's tools and other articles will always be a reflection of that person's needs. And the true intention behind split-twig figurines, the layers of cultural mandates and beliefs, will never be known.

A team was assembled in the mid-1950s to study split-twig figurines of the Grand Canyon. The conclusion was that "these caves were used for the purpose of ceremonial hunting magic, where, preparatory to the hunt, small animal models were made from split twigs, taken to certain sacred inaccessible caves and ritually killed, buried, or otherwise magically annihilated in order to insure success in the coming hunt."

Since then, evidence suggests that twigs were carried up and figurines were constructed inside the caves. Often whole and split twigs are found in the dim recesses. These unfinished pieces were not strewn about. They appear to be deliberately placed.

Inside some of these caves are the bones and droppings of animals that died in the Grand Canyon as long as 45,000 years before the figurines were crafted and placed. Found were the remains of condors and bighorn sheep, as well as mountain goat and ground sloth species that became extinct toward the end of the last ice age. The makers of split-twig figurines would have puzzled over these fossil bones and droppings, not recognizing them. The skull of a Harrington's mountain goat, with its short, black horns and its unfamiliar arrangement of teeth, must have baffled them.

Some archaeologists speak of relationships between the fossil bones, the droppings, and the small human artifacts.

The Archaic painting of a deer.

Caves lacking in fossils also tend to be lacking in figurines.

I once spoke with Jim Mead, a researcher from Northern Arizona Univeristy, about the bones in these caves. At the time, we were working on a cave excavation of Pleistocene mammals in Colorado. While we tinkered with tweezers through the limbs of 2-million-year-old rabbits and the teeth of horses, Mead told me about what he had seen when he was working in the Grand Canyon. He had entered many of the caves, counted the dung of extinct sloths, and painstakingly excavated, examined, and then just as painstakingly replaced the figurines of Archaic age. He has been one of the principal theorists on the relationship between the figurines and the bones, and as he described this relationship, his eyes grew bright. He believes that each rock cairn, regardless of the number of figurines contained within, belonged to an individual who placed the figurines and constructed it.

"I have no factual evidence at all," he said with a shrug.

Most archaeologists speak of the Archaics in such terms. They have beliefs and feelings but not substantiating information.

Mead complained of vandalism, mentioning that hundreds, if not thousands, of figurines have been stolen. But what seems to weigh heavier on him than the thefts is that people have entered many of the accessible caves and rearranged the placement of figurines. This is the greatest of desecrations, because the patterns left by the Archaics were so exact and rich with implication.

He told me about ledges upon which cairns were constructed around the periphery of the room, their placement making a design or a map.

"Even the Anasazi were vandals," he said. "Whenever a cave shows sign of Anasazi occupation, the place is disheveled, the older cairns dismembered or toppled. If the cave belonged only to the Archaic, then it was neatly arranged."

It is the night before the full moon. Only a missing sliver of light keeps it from being full. Thunderstorms roam the canyons. I can hear them and see the quick blue of their far-off lightning. I walk along a bench from my camp, planning to reach the rock art panel. The moon should have it illuminated by now. A cloudburst falls from the rim. Its weight can be felt as it hits. Sudden wind and horizontal rain. Every plant bends down at once. Even the solid junipers. I always run in storms like this. It seems like the thing to do with all this motion and suddenness. Sometimes, I run for a shelter. Sometimes, I just run. The canyon goes dark as the moon blanks out, and I sprint down the bench, taking shelter in the overhang of painted figures. It will be mostly dry in here, even with

the wind. Mist gets blown in, washed one way, then another. There is not enough light to see any of the paintings, so I crouch and face outward. Curtains of water come at once, sealing off the front of the alcove an arm's length away.

Rocks remain hot from the day, so the rain smells like steam and sandstone. The junipers smell a bit like gin. The storm lasts maybe six minutes. Then it ends. I do not move. The sheet of water dwindles to five waterfalls, then braids into a bunch of strands that I can catch with my hands. The moon shows a bit, scattering light like hand-torn quilt squares all over the canyon.

What I see in the floor of the canyon at first makes no sense. There is motion down there. A broad white band, looking like milk spilled from a vat, is rolling across the floor. The illusion advances through the canyon, pausing in places, moving ahead in others. It is too solid and deliberate for mere moonlight. It seems that my eyes are tricking me.

Then, I realize the canyon is flooding. The sound I am hearing is not wind. The leading edge of the flood is gathering moonlight along with branches, mud, and rocks. The light of the moon spreads beyond the flood, filling the entire canyon as the clouds break. I can hear the tumbling of rocks.

The light arrives, and the full chamber behind me turns a creamy blue. Still squatting on my haunches, I look back, peering across my shoulder into the room. Painted figures stand in reflected moonlight, curving over my head. They are pulled taut against the rock face. Suddenly, I am severed from time. No, they are not like ghosts. They seem more alive than that. Torsos and heads stand clearer in the moonlight than I had thought they would. I turn my head down, then rise and walk away. A person can ask for only so much.

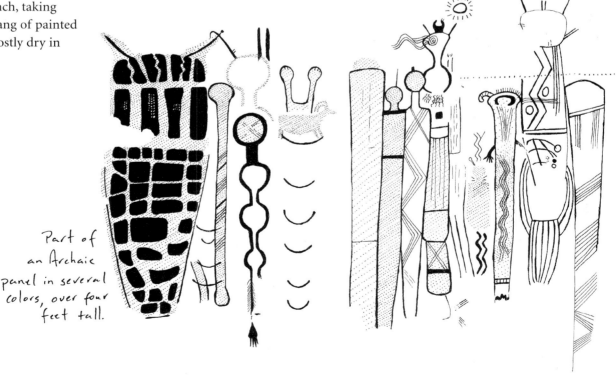

Part of an Archaic panel in several colors, over four feet tall.

THE GRANDEST GORGE

WHERE DOES THE GRANDEST PART OF GRAND CANYON BEGIN?
SOME MARK THE SPOT AT NANKOWEAP, A LITTLE MORE THAN 50 RIVER
miles into the Canyon. Others place the point about 10 miles farther along, where the Little Colorado River flows into the Colorado River. Some choose Tanner Rapids, where the Colorado decisively turns west to breach the East Kaibab Monocline.

I place the start at the Little Colorado, because just downstream from the confluence the orderly array of flat-lying strata abruptly ends. In its place, the youngest of the Precambrian rocks rise from the river and form beds that stand out because they are tilted. And they are much older, about a billion years old, than the rocks they supplant.

A little farther down, the Canyon opens to the sky. The rims build higher. Then, about 77 miles from Lees Ferry, the Colorado plunges through Hance Rapids and beyond there into ancient black rocks twisted and contorted by titanic forces unimaginable. With these clues for an introduction, the Colorado River has crossed a threshold into the grandest segment of the Canyon: the classic Grand Canyon. The entire nature of the inner Canyon has transformed.

A hundred years ago, most visitors to Grand Canyon gravitated to the South Rim within a few miles of today's Grand Canyon Village. The reasons were compelling then, and they remain so today. There, about 90 river miles from Lees Ferry, the Canyon achieves its greatest depth, the surrounding forest its most primeval expression, and, viewed from the Rim, the Canyon landforms are as sublime as any on earth. Mighty temples rise from the Canyon's foundations, profound tributaries plunge from rim to river, and tiers of cliffs rise like steps from desert floor to alpine rim.

At river level, rapids like none before arrive in quick succession: Sockdolager, Grapevine, Horn Creek, Granite, Hermit, Crystal. Upper Granite Gorge bristles with unscalable crags and impenetrable canyons. The river landscape is stark, pure, intractable, and harsh. Little of this can be perceived from the Rim.

At first acquaintance, the classic realm of the Grand Canyon in Upper Granite Gorge is menacing and sinister; yet with further familiarity, this environment — although it reverberates with unseen forces — becomes more monumental than menacing and more awesome than sinister.

Opposite: Turquoise waters of the Little Colorado River cascade toward the Colorado River and the start of the Canyon's grandest gorge.

Little Colorado River Gorge

Left: The Little Colorado River cascades over travertine dams upstream of the Salt Trail, used by native peoples to reach salt deposits on the Colorado River.

Above: In June, shrinking pools and silky mud present fading evidence of spring floods. This site lies 15 miles downstream from Cameron on the Navajo Indian Reservation.

Joining Forces

Opposite: Just above its confluence with the Colorado River, the Little Colorado cascades over a series of parapets formed from the mineral travertine.

Left: On the benches above the Canyon floor, greenstem paperflower blooms in June.

Below: An eyebrow of Tapeats sandstone glowers over the Little Colorado River at its sunlit confluence with the Colorado River.

Above: Rust-stained Lava Creek merges with the Colorado River after a September downpour.

Clouds Cast an Influence

Right: Clouds and mist subdue the Canyon's colors and obscure Comanche Point, viewed from Lava Canyon (Chuar) Rapids.

Following panel: The summit of Coronado Butte disappears into a halo of clouds in September.

Moving Into Granite Gorge

Opposite: Acting as a vise, Upper Granite Gorge squeezes the Colorado River upstream from Grapevine Rapids.

Left: Cascading water rushes between boulders at the head of Nevills Rapids, River Mile 75.

Below: September storm clouds engulf the South Rim and sweep out over the Canyon downstream from Tanner Rapids.

Below: Clear Creek bounces over the Sideways Waterfall.

Falling Toward the River

Right: Cottonwood trees line the course of Clear Creek a few miles upstream of its confluence with the Colorado.

Opposite: Cheyava Falls bursts to life in the spring when rising temperatures assault deep winter snows blanketing the North Rim.

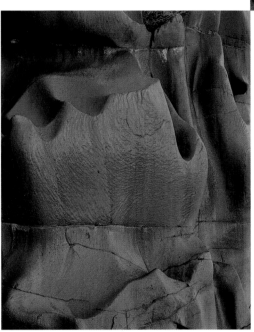

Opposite: Dana Butte looms over the Colorado River at Granite Falls Rapids.

The Sculptures of Granite Gorge

Left: The metallic color and liquid form of Vishnu schist reflect blue sky and green river upstream from Clear Creek Canyon.

Above: Swirling currents and eons of floods have carved and shaped Vishnu schist near Zoroaster Canyon.

Before the Fall

Following panel: Craggy granite constrains the Colorado River as it approaches a 17-foot plunge through Granite Falls Rapids.

A SENSE
OF
STONE

EACH KIND OF ROCK CAN CHANGE YOUR MOOD. NOT IN SOME SUBTLE, SUBLIMINAL WAY, BUT LIKE A SUDDEN TURN OF EMOTIONS. LIKE A SLAP IN THE face, then a kiss on the back of the neck. Sand will rub differently in your boots. One night it will provide good dreams; another, nightmares. You will grow meditative on the rims of the Esplanade sandstone, with all of the open light and long vistas, then become wild-eyed and tense in the dusky narrows of Redwall limestone. Each of your sensations will be scratched down to whatever formation lies below your hands or feet.

ROCK DOWN HERE IS EXTRAVAGANT, KNEADED IN EVERY DIRECTION, MIXED WITH ANY OTHER ROCK ON HAND. THIS WHOLE MATRIX WAS PRESSED INTO THE PLANET, HEATED TO 700° CELSIUS, AND TWISTED LIKE TAFFY.

Down here in the lowest, darkest rock, I cannot help but feel that the Colorado River cut too deeply into the earth, that it exposed stone never meant to see the light of day. The river comes in from my right shoulder, leaves by my left, running determinedly through this shoebox canyon. The rock that is cut is Vishnu schist. It is a fabric of dark Precambrian rock, 1.7 billion years old, fiercely solid. I am perched on an outcrop; I came all the way down this canyon but can't quite reach the river 50 feet below. There is a kind of fear in the pit of these jet black canyons. It is the fear of being watched or hunted by something much more cunning and capable than myself. I don't know if it is an intrinsic fear of sudden floods or just

Opposite: A backpacker, perhaps searching for a reasonable route down, stands on a brow of Redwall limestone jutting over Buck Farm Canyon, which joins the Colorado River at the base of the far cliff.

a stray chill. It brings my observations to the forefront. I watch everything carefully, as if it mattered.

I have come with three others. I can see two of them, hunting for ways down to the river. Another is sitting alone where I cannot see her. We joined each other eight days ago. I had come out to resupply and take a few days' rest midway along a walk from Tanner Canyon to the Aztec Amphitheater of Royal Arch Creek, a slowly walked route that will take 40 days. Twelve days remain.

Very little of the Grand Canyon bears likeness to the remainder of the Colorado Plateau. Elsewhere, say in Southeast Utah, the earth is bulging. There, you will stop at a dead end in Navajo sandstone where curves take to the sky. In juxtaposition, the Grand Canyon has sharply terraced structures where, if you become blocked, it will not be at a majestically cusped and echoing amphitheater, but at a narrow crack with a 40-ton boulder jammed over your head. The Grand Canyon is hard, biting. Routes resign themselves between cliffs, cliffs that are scattered everywhere.

This Vishnu schist is the hardest of the formations, the final statement at the bottom of the Grand Canyon. Try to follow the topography of this schist with your eyes. It is trickery. Picking out a canyon is like trying to find a speckled plover egg among brown stones. When I first became surrounded by the schist in Grapevine Canyon weeks ago, it was like a hall of mirrors, with dark flanges and corkscrewed hallways. There is no other rock like this in the Canyon, nothing so

baffling. What looks like a cliff is a canyon. A cleft easily 10 feet wide becomes no wider than a hand. You walk through these inner canyons the way you turn pages in a murder mystery — looking over your shoulder, unable to put it down, not sure of what the next twist might be.

It is partially the gloss of the schist that causes this visual effect. It involves its dungeon darkness, its sharp-angled patterns of erosion, and its shift in colors from olive to brown to a reddish black verging on burnt blood. Often, what is considered to be a single formation actually may have manifold origins and textures.

By the late 1800s, the entire metamorphic basement of the Grand Canyon was known simply as Vishnu, which since has been divided into the Vishnu metamorphic complex, Zoroaster plutonic complex, Trinity gneiss, and Elves Chasm gneiss, plus a host of other minor formations. Most other formations of the Canyon tend toward structural simplicity, easily layered like book pages.

This rock down here is extravagant, kneaded in every direction, mixed with any other rock on hand. Depending on the regional forces of metamorphism, and on the type of rock being heated and folded, different types of schist, gneiss, and slate were formed. The glistening, flaking mica and quartz schists emerged from what once were sedimentary rocks, while the darker, more pure schists developed from volcanic rocks. The volcanic segments originally were

ash and lava flows, perhaps remnants of island chains much like the Aleutian or the Hawaiian islands. Around these islands were quartz-rich sediments of sand, silt, and clay. This whole matrix was pressed into the planet, heated to 700° Celsius, and twisted like taffy.

Thrown into this mix are brightly colored swarms of volcanic plutons, dikes, and sills that broke into the hard Vishnu rocks just as the heaviest metamorphic activity ended, about 1.5 billion years ago.

At river level, where all of these rocks are scrubbed together, the granite set into the schist is as red and polished as a black widow's hourglass. Some of the walls are tightly laced with these Zoroaster granites, and even they vary markedly in color and grain. There are bands only inches wide and those that

Some rock formations of the Grand Canyon

consume canyon floors for five or six miles. Some of the intrusions broke their way into the schist at the peak of metamorphism, becoming properly convoluted, while others escaped metamorphism, maintaining their original shapes. Quartz, being slowest to cool and harden, sank to the center of these internal, molten streams, so that now you find pure, white quartz inlaid into pink and red bands of Zoroaster. This builds illusions.

It looks like madness down here. Darkness and suddenness, canyons that wind themselves tight down to the river. When we walk back along the side canyon, black walls of schist soar over us like ravens.

I have found it more reasonable to carry a geologic map than a topographic map here. A topographic map is a field of lines showing the elevation of local terrain in 40-foot intervals. Forty feet is not enough. All the necessary routes are the length of your arm or are hinged off of boulders that don't appear on maps. Geologic maps look like abstract paintings. (I've seen them hung on living room walls.) Each color represents a formation viewed from above, so that the region is a sea of colors as various formations come to the surface. The colors themselves are a meaningless display until you have studied the tendencies of each formation — how the rocks feel to the touch, how well a piece will stay as a handhold.

Approaching the map's bluish green of Tapeats sandstone, you know that in the brief couple of hundred feet of cliff (which shows few features on a topo map), you will at least have a chance of getting down, that the Tapeats is built of firm ledges where you can lower yourself, slinging your gear down, clambering behind. The drab green map color of the Coconino sandstone means that you will have to walk for some time, maybe for miles or even days, trying to find a crack that takes you up or down. Handholds in the unexfoliated schist will be firm. Those in the Dox sandstone will come apart like pastry. Redwall limestone in a canyon floor will be smooth as a cowrie shell, while the same limestone lying in the open against rain and wind will be sharp as a cheese grater and will tear skin.

AFTER DAYS INSIDE THE HYPNOTIC waves of schist, we eventually emerge onto one of the interior rims, the roof of Esplanade sandstone where we can spread our arms and breathe against the wide sky. On this evening, we gather food and supplies at a cache, treating ourselves to fresh garlic and olive oil in pasta, to single-malt whisky sipped as the sun drops and warm clothes come on. Dusk light lingers with a gentle, powdery glow. The seasons have changed. November has brought a solid coolness. Mornings and evenings now are sharp with cold.

When I met my partners for this leg of the hike to Royal Arch Creek, we walked down between Redwall limestone cliffs as light, early November snow turned to mist, dusting our faces and shoulders. That day, one of my companions came with me along a small drainage where we found water holes in the Supai formation. Rain runoff had gathered in the slick, flood-scoured cavities in the floor, as it does so well in the resistant, red sandstones of this formation. Down on all fours, lips to the water. He said he had never done it before, drunk straight off the rock. He came up with water dripping down his chin. Baptized.

Beyond our cache, the heads of small canyons pinch against higher cliffs, sending us into steep cascades of Hermit shale. The damp shale darkens our boots with a deep red. Over our heads looms the white of the Coconino sandstone. We each look up now and then, taken by vertigo, by the sweeping crossbed lines of the Coconino that arc into the sky and turn into high cirrus clouds. Every stab of cliff that rises high enough in the Grand Canyon is crossbanded by the Coconino, a strong white sandstone prominent against surrounding rusts and pastels. It is the first formation to warm in the morning, the last to hold light at dusk. It is the remnant of great coastal dunes, where impurities were winnowed out by constant ocean winds, leaving this raw quartz sand to compact eventually into a pure sandstone. One of the more striking contrasts in the Canyon is the one between the Coconino sandstone cliffs and the slopes of Hermit shale below. White and curry-beige walls stand on red, inarticulate shelves. The polarity is striking.

This partnering of massive, solid formations and weak ledges is what gives the Grand Canyon its famous visual terraces. Using unorthodox optimism, geologists refer to cliff-forming rocks such as the Coconino as "competent." The weak mudstones and siltstones of the Hermit are "incompetent." The

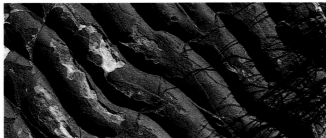

Above: Erosion has left a Kaibab limestone sculpture teetering at the edge of the North Rim.

Geological Patterns of Erosion

From Top Left: With a cobble of granite resting in a pocket, blades and fins of Vishnu schist form a rugged composition at river's edge.

This fluted and polished rock is Vishnu schist in the Lower Granite Gorge.

Ripple marks, usually formed by gentle, shallow-water currents, are frozen in sandstone in the Little Colorado River Gorge.

A slab of Coconino sandstone in Soap Creek Canyon fell and shattered into a chaotic arrangement.

grains of the Coconino were carefully packed by winds, sorted as if a gem glass had been used, granules placed with fine tweezers so that they would fit neatly into each other. This homogeneity gives the rock strength against erosion, allowing it to wear like a statue. You see this in the Coconino, the Redwall, and, to a lesser extent, the Supai and Tapeats. These cliffs are interrupted by the talus-ridden slopes of Hermit shale, Bright Angel shale, and Dox sandstone, where the formations are too weak to hold themselves together or to support the cliffs overhead. The cliffs cave into huge blocks, littering the slopes below. This arrangement is what you gaze upon from the Rim. It is the stark, striking angles of cliffs and steps that invite lithograph artists who use straightedges as painting tools.

Our walking slows toward the end of the day as we drop from the Hermit shale to the Supai and, below, take ledges into deepening canyons. Backpacks are sent down on webbing. We drop into the Redwall limestone where we hold our breath. Light turns gray, mingling with the scoured cliffs of blue limestone. Shoulders and packs rub on rock because the walls have come together, almost touching. There is no more room. The sky closes. Again, emotions shift.

There is the waiting, 5 or 10 minutes as someone climbs down, cumbersome with a large pack. As the canyon narrows, sounds arrive. Sounds of fingers sweeping pebbles from handholds, the slow bustling of gear, tightly exhaled breaths on the downclimb. The nervous laugh. The quiet voice. Stephanie reaches out to brace my foot. I lower some webbing

Josh can use as a hold. Mike braces Stephanie with his shoulder. We become gymnasts of the Redwall.

Redwall limestone is red only where the Supai formation and the Hermit shale have been leaking iron oxide. That is the color of the big cliffs: rain-driven rust. Inside the canyons, the rock is worn to its native color, that of an overcast sky. The Redwall is the monumental formation of the Grand Canyon. It dominates almost every view from the Rim, looking like the Great Wall of China going in and out of each canyon below. These folded robes of cliffs are a barrier to everything except birds and wind-carried seeds.

Historic and prehistoric trails (often, the same) depend on a break in the Redwall to reach from the river to the Rim. Harvey Butchart, a man who has walked more than 15,000 miles in the Grand Canyon, logged 164 routes through the Redwall limestone. Most of the routes are across tough exposures and into cracks. One, near Enfilade Point, eluded him for 10 years. But Butchart knew it was there. He had heard about a route once used by Supai Indians farming the delta at Fossil Bay Canyon.

He tells the story of approaching a Supai man who had just emerged from a sweat bath. The man got out his glasses, with only one lens intact, still covered in sweat, to examine Butchart's map. "I don't know, maybe he didn't understand maps," said Butchart, now in his 90s. "Anyway, he said he couldn't remember, he was too small a boy, but his father had

taken him down there. So that left me pretty much in the dark."

So Butchart tried spotting from an airplane to find the right crack. Then he trekked into the Canyon repeatedly on foot.

"I found I could get down this break in the Redwall, although in one place I had to face in and go down ledges with hands and toes. Where there was a big chockstone, I had to go bypassing it and found out I could get across to where I'd already been from the bottom up. So I completed that trip through there. Called it the Enfilade Point route."

The routes in the Redwall are either cracks and natural stair steps down the massive cliffs, or they are passages through canyons such as this. The shape of a canyon is determined by the particular formation on the floor. If the floor is of Hermit shale, then the canyon will be wide, having broken into a weak layer that erodes laterally, giving space to shout. If the floor is like this, Redwall limestone, the cut is narrow and sheer. You keep your voice low. When, eventually, this canyon is carved through the hard limestones and into the loose Bright Angel shale below, it will pitch outward.

For now, we are in the limestone, wading through the accumulated water of springs, our packs hiked up onto our shoulders so they don't get wet, boots tied off as we go barefoot. Western redbud trees hug the walls, along with the low, crowded leaves of snapdragon, crimson monkeyflower, and yellow columbine yet to bloom. Camp is set, hanging like an ornament among great ledges where the canyon contacts Bright

Angel shale and walls fall apart, no longer held sturdy by the Redwall. The canyon drops below among towers, archways, and stairways where waterfalls plunge. The place looks like a geologic rummage sale. Spare cliffs, theatrical skylines, boulders left over from floods. The cleanness and definition of solid limestone has ended.

This is Thanksgiving Day and, after the sun has set, we bring our sleeping bags together and eat a meal of rice and spices. Evening slides away as we watch, stealing the light and all knowledge of upstream and downstream. Finally, the only element of direction remaining is the sound of the small creek. The sound is evidence that in this thrusting, toppling canyon there is order. The soft, persistent sough of water.

In the morning, we rappel a short distance and work down into the Bright Angel shale. Colors in the shale (where you are able to find the shale exposed from beneath crashed limestone of overhead cliffs) are not repeated elsewhere in the Canyon. Mostly it is pale green, a green you can see clearly from the Rim. Viewed from the top, the Bright Angel forms an apron throughout the Canyon, a place where you can walk in full view of the highest rims. The shale layer is the softest object to touch your eyes, from miles away looking like it is being poured. The green comes mostly from the mineral glauconite, which resides in many of the formation's shales. Up close, though, the glauconite does not dominate. Up close, you are looking at a spilled box of paints.

Talk with people about rocks in the Grand Canyon and you will not often hear of the Bright Angel shale. It is one of the incompetents. Even pleasing to the eye, it is not why you come to stare at the Canyon. It is not one of the bold, terrifying cliffs. It does not offer an adventurous climb, only a sloped platform on which to walk and a good place to sleep if you wish to be blanketed in stars. But it is a visual anchor in the Canyon's configuration. You will hear of it from artists. I once spoke to Bruce Aiken, a painter living and working inside the Canyon for 26 years. No other formation gripped him so much.

"When you get down onto the Bright Angel shale and tramp around on it, you start seeing the yellow and the purple with the green," he said. "And when those three colors come together, they're really beautiful, when you put them next to each other. Yellow and purple, anyway, are opposites on the color wheel — what's called complementary colors in the world of art. When you put purple and yellow next to each other, you've got a vibrating situation. The colors vibrate, literally; it just sets up tension. Think about baseball uniforms. The New York Mets have blue and orange piping on their uniforms. Those are also opposites on the color wheel. That kind of thing is done a lot in sports or in advertising. It's attractive. I see it when I'm walking along the trail. I see it. I'm not just walking through there and thinking about something else. Sometimes I see it to the point where I have to bend down and do something. I physically want to hold it. Here, I was hiking in and I picked this up." Digging into his pocket, Bruce unloaded bits of rock, fantastic bits of green and purple that do not seem possible for rocks. "I had to pick them up."

They scattered across the table, little pieces of fascination. Living in a house situated in the Bright Angel shale for decades, he still could not help but run fingers across the formation, rotating its pieces around in his hands every day.

There are baby blues, too. Layers of an applesauce color and fresh-cut beets and the inky purple of black bean juice. One small layer within the Bright Angel shale, only about four inches thick, holds a crumbly, luminous mudstone, too weak to make an actual rock. It comes apart like dry bread in the hand. It is the color of a red wine stain on a white tablecloth, yet if you look closely, you can see a sheen, the kind of lustrous shine you get from beetle carapaces. Rubbed between fingers, it becomes a pigment and adheres to the skin. I rubbed this across my arms and legs once, and the soft blush stayed for two days. Bruce Aiken says his daughters used to paint themselves with it and run and scream with delight. "My girls would be coming home with it covering their bodies," he says. "Stark, buck-naked five- and seven-year-olds, bodies just painted with the stuff."

The shale certainly is variegated, but it also is a tactile formation, riddled with trilobite and worm tracks left in fine mud about 300 million years ago. The trace fossils of burrows and drag marks were left in a mud once so fine that if you had set your hand down that long ago, your fingerprints would now show as fossils. These are accompanied by the fossils of primitive mollusks,

Records of Life

The sedimentary rocks of the Grand Canyon, shale, sandstone, and limestone, archive a record of life from hundreds of millions of years ago.

Above: Maidenhair ferns wreathe a slab of Tapeats sandstone, its surface knotted with fucoids, which may be fossilized worm burrows.

From Top Right: A primeval shell near the Rim.

A fossil etched in Kaibab limestone.

Crinoid stems, the remains of tiny marine creatures, are embedded in Kaibab limestone.

Eroded crinoid stems fill a visitor's palm.

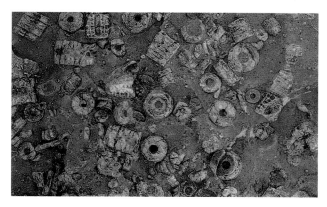

echinoderms, sponges, algae, and trilobites. But mostly what can be seen are these jumbles of traces. There is enough detail that individual shapes have acquired their own nomenclature, the same way an animal will be named by species and genus. The mark of a trilobite at rest is *Rusophycus*, while one in motion is *Cruziana*. This can become so specific as to be offered a full title such as *Cruziana arizonensis*, which is the track of a mobile trilobite found in layers just below the Bright Angel shale.

At the downslope tip of the Bright Angel shale is the Tapeats sandstone. The shale simply hits this firm, brown platform, then a sheer drop of several hundred feet lies beyond. Whenever a canyon passes through this sandstone, it squints, just for a moment, just long enough — a couple hundred vertical feet — to change the entire topography. The revealing sunlight and layered pastels of the Bright Angel close into narrow darkness, into sandstone hues of coffee and cranberries. The narrows of Deer Creek and Blacktail Canyon, the big waterfall on Stone Creek, the perfectly straight stream of a waterfall in Red Canyon, these are all classic effects of the Tapeats negotiating with a stream course, where tall chutes of carved rock drop into shade, then suddenly open into whichever formation is there. Below, the Tapeats is an unconformity, a plain of rock eroded and now missing from the sequence. Because of this, the next formation is sometimes the Vishnu schist, sometimes is Dox sandstone, depending on what was last eroded before the Tapeats sandstone was dropped into place. The Tapeats is the threshold.

WE DECIDE TO SCATTER INTO THIS rock. The agreement is that we will meet the next day at Copper Canyon. But for now we go free, looking for our own places, for brief tastes of solitude. The Tapeats is a good place for this. A hide-and-seek formation, it breaks into ledges like stacks of cardboard. I walk for most of the day along its rim before setting camp, a camp that hangs nearly a thousand feet above the Colorado River. The river breaks around shields of lifted Zoroaster granite where Waltenberg Rapids bathes the cliffs in a steady roaring. It is a perfect place to sleep. The lulling sound of Waltenberg and the flatness of these stone planks with ceilings overhead. In the Tapeats, there always will be a level place for my back, a burrow to crawl into.

Tapeats was deposited about 500 million years ago, mostly in the form of streams spilling across tidal regions, hauling pebbles and coarse-grained sands to the sea. Kernels of rusted, orange grains stand from the rock's

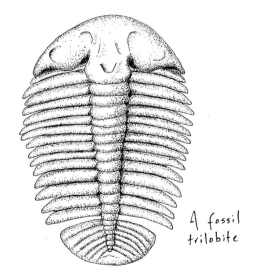

A fossil trilobite

surface. The passing of different sizes of creeks and different sources of materials can be seen in the sediments left behind. Larger grains imply larger flows and you can follow with your fingers exactly how and where these sediments were abandoned. Groundwater moving through the porous sandstone has precipitated iron oxide, which now appears as fluid, purple bands. These iron oxide designs — styles more common to the backs of seashells than to rocks — pass vertically, ignoring the boundaries of the original streams and their original sand. It is a good place to sit, reading through words written all over the sandstone.

As I read the next morning, I turn to see two big rocks in the air, fallen from the top of the Redwall. As they turn, they show their pale undersides the way fish flash their bellies in the water. Two feet across, maybe three. They vanish behind an outcrop of Bright Angel shale. Seconds later I hear the impact. Sharp cracks. Echoes.

AFTER WE MEET IN COPPER Canyon, we move on, and in coming days we cross all of these formations, walking out to the Rim where my truck is parked. The Rim, the uppermost formation, the farthest from Vishnu schist in color, shape and distance, is the Kaibab formation. It is the roof of the Grand Canyon, presenting itself as a cliff, as sharpened hoodoo towers, and as slopes dressed in piñons, junipers, and cliffrose.

From east to west the formation changes noticeably. It consists of about 75 percent sandstone at the far east near Desert View and nearly all limestone to the west. This has to do with it being formed from an ocean floor, influenced greatly by its proximity to a coast. The western shore of a continent once ran between Holbrook, Arizona, and southeastern Utah, leaving the region that would become the Grand Canyon submerged in a shallow sea.

At an archive, I once examined a 1934 sketch by Edwin McKee, who then held the job of park naturalist at Grand Canyon. He titled his paper "Common Fossils of Open Seas During Kaibab Times" and drew six mollusk shells that he had gathered. Careful observation had been made of the smallest details, the roundness of a marble-sized *Composita* and the 66 radiating lines of a broad *Derbya*. He drew them as he found them, with their roughened edges, using dotted lines to suggest their shapes prior to erosion. At the bottom of the page, McKee had drawn a cross section of the Kaibab formation from one end of the Grand Canyon to the other, showing how more brackish-water fossils appear in the sandstones to the east, while marine fossils dominate the limestone-riddled west.

McKee implied that streams off the land once entered the Kaibab Sea from the east, turning the water brackish and depositing sand. Meanwhile, the west remained far offshore and without fresh stream water, gathering a different biota entirely. He wrote, "It is hoped that this brief sketch of certain conditions in the Kaibab sea will give something of a picture, and one of reasonable accuracy, of a small part of that most unusual and remarkable period, the Permian." The paper was yellowed, but well kept and still firm to the touch, a fossil itself.

Moving slowly through the shade of piñon trees, up through packs of snow kept frozen on the cold north-facing Rim, we reach the top edge of the Kaibab formation within half an hour of each other. I stop before clearing the Rim, watching the dawn. Then sunrise floods into the Grand Canyon below. Cold this morning. I pull out my journal. I am sloppy with the pen — even with the fingers of my gloves cut off — as I back against a juniper trunk, propping my journal between my knees. The first sunlight comes haunting the Coconino sandstone. The rock appears saturated with cadmium in the first couple minutes of light, then surrenders intensity to the formations below. Rows of Redwall unfold as the sun works inside of each available canyon.

I take out the topographic map and look at the route just completed. I have never traveled in a place with so many alluring names as the Grand Canyon. Names crowd the map. I find different landmarks with my finger, places I have circled on this walk. It is fascinating yet disturbing to see so many names. A sequence of side canyons — Topaz, Slate, Agate, Sapphire, Turquoise, Ruby, Serpentine, Copper, and Garnet — are named more from convenience than from any notable aspect of each canyon. The points that reach farthest out from the South Rim are named for Native American tribes. Landmarks gathered in certain regions are named after Eastern religions or after Spanish explorers. From these appelations, the moods of John Wesley Powell or government cartographers can be deciphered better than the moods of the landmarks themselves.

Studying this map, I think that when a map looks more like a dictionary than a landscape, we have misunderstood something important about the place. Still, inside of these canyons we bleed when we fall, and we still sleep like children when cradled by boulders. Even considering the maps and names we've made, the depth of our innocence here startles me.

I put away the journal, fold the map. The Grand Canyon possesses a largeness that does not translate into cubes or feet or titles. No common dimensions are stored here. It is in stillness like this, when sunlight reaches into the Canyon, that the size becomes most tangible. It is not the proportions given on a piece of paper, the length and width of the place. It is the knowledge we have about each stone we have touched. I try to remember as I watch the sunlight, try to remember the contrasting feel of the rocks. This is when I have some sense of what is down there. More than can be mapped. All the categories are shed into individual stones that we weighed in our hands. Familiarity comes from a kneecap scraped across the toughened surface of a Redwall boulder. These are the contents of the Grand Canyon.

CHAMBERS IN THE ROCK

ADVENTURERS TRAVELING BY FOOT OR BOAT ENTER ANOTHER WORLD WHEN THEY ENTER THE GRAND CANYON'S INTERIOR.

Stand at the edge of the Colorado River and look around. A map suggests that you are but a few miles from the cool, forested plateau that lies out of sight behind cliffs or crags. But your senses insist that the familiar rims are beyond reach, that distances measured in miles are not accurate.

At the bottom, the Grand Canyon smells different, sounds different, looks different. It is different.

Although they can glimpse the Colorado, those who look with binoculars from the Rim cannot sense the river's power surging through a landscape of desolate, elemental, and inhospitable harshness.

Hidden from prying eyes on the Rim and the unobservant at the river are astonishing refuges from the harsh light and noisy drama along the river corridor. There, in the side canyons, are the gems of the Grand Canyon.

Walking away from the river's edge, stepping over the boulders, pushing through a screen of tamarisks and making way toward a cleft in the wall, you'll find that another world materializes. The boom of the river subsides and in a few minutes the entire enfolding world measures only a few yards wide. The echoes of footfalls, the giggles of a streamlet, the patter of seep-waters fill the microcosm.

Elves Chasm initiates an astonishing series of oases hidden in the cliffs. Blacktail Canyon, Stone Creek, Tapeats, Deer Creek, Kanab, Olo, Matkatamiba, Havasu, Tuckup, National, Fern Glen, Cove, and many other niches whisper their siren songs: The fragrance of flowers and ferns and the sound of trickling water are irresistible.

Many are shady, watered, silent, intimate, secluded, tranquil, and screened from the tumultuous river world. The Grand Canyon environment has collapsed to the size of a comfortable room of peace and soothing silence.

Even the river corridor narrows to a kind of intimacy along the final third of this river segment. Some call it the Muav Gorge. Its entrance is found at Kanab Canyon and it meanders on for 30 miles, gently curving left, then right, almost undisturbed by raucous cataracts. The gorge marks the final peaceful domain of the tranquil stone chambers.

Opposite: Spools of watery ribbons unwind between travertine boulders in Elves Chasm as spring brings melted snow to the Canyon's waterways.

Hidden in the Cliffs

Opposite: Royal Arch Creek trickles quietly beneath its namesake to begin a swift descent into Elves Chasm. The creek joins the Colorado below River Mile 116.

Left: Maidenhair ferns nod their welcome in the cool confines of the upper chambers of Elves Chasm on a July morning.

Above: An acacia tree leans out over a cliff near the entrance to Elves Chasm.

A Canyon Gash

Following panel: Silky sheets of water ripple through the Shinumo Narrows of remote Stone Creek on a March afternoon. The site is about three miles up from the Colorado on the north side, and the creek joins the river near Mile 132.

Opposite: Through a series of waterfall grottos, Stone Creek leaves a trail of mosses, ferns, and plunge pools on its way to the Colorado River.

Trails of Water

Above: The September sun entangles itself in the branches of a cottonwood tree along Tapeats Creek.

Left: Deer Creek drops from "the patio" into Deer Creek Gorge.

Flowing Through Stone

Opposite: Spared by the flash floods, a redbud tree clings to a mound of cobbles tucked into a niche along Deer Creek.

Above: Billows of water tumble into the dim depths of Deer Creek Gorge on the Canyon's north side.

Oases

Right: A blooming sacred datura and an evening primrose plant hug the base of a scorched cottonwood tree in Deer Creek Valley.

Below: Deer Creek Spring bursts from limestone caverns to plunge 30 feet, hammering the boulders and nourishing the vegetation.

Rubble

Opposite: Boulders and gravel carpet the floor of Jumpup Canyon, a tributary of Kanab Canyon on the north side of the Colorado. Kanab, in turn, sends its water to the Colorado, meeting it near River Mile 143.

Tributaries to the Colorado

Opposite: Crystalline pools display a basin littered with pebbles in Olo Canyon.

Left: Matkatamiba Creek below the South Rim takes leave of a soaring alcove and heads for an appointment with the Colorado River.

Below: Now dry, Fern Glen Canyon at times sends runoff water to the Colorado.

Matkatamiba Creek

Above: Chutes, chambers, and interlocking walls grip Matkatamiba Creek in its upper reaches above the Colorado River, while Arizona grapes lean out from the ledges above.

Opposite: The Colorado River swirls by the mouth of Matkatamiba Creek (not visible in the photo) at River Mile 148.

Natural Dams in Havasu Canyon

Following panel: Pools of water form behind dams cemented with the mineral travertine (calcium carbonate) at the foot of Mooney Falls on Havasu Creek — about a 5.5-mile hike from the Colorado River. Travertine deposits on the creek's bed cause the stream to mirror the surrounding greens and browns of Havasu Canyon, lending the water a unique color.

Rhapsody in Blue-Green

Opposite: A mile or so above Mooney Falls on Havasu Creek, the tandem cascades of Havasu Falls plunge into a lagoon on the Havasupai Indian Reservation.

Above: Resembling folds of a massive curtain, the walls over which the waterfalls drop represent the work of geology and hydrology. Dissolved travertine carried by the water coats the rock in shaggy layers. This formation is on Mooney Falls.

Above: Pools, boulders, and reflections elbow one another for space in the cramped quarters of Tuckup Canyon on the north side of the Colorado River.

Tuckup Canyon

Right: Morning light illuminates the river corridor at Mile 164.

FOLLOWING
BIGHORN

WITH ONE HEADLAMP TURNED ON IN A NIGHT SNOWSTORM, IT'S HARD NOT TO GET DIZZY. THE DANCE OF FLAKES LOOKS LIKE A swarm of bees in a spotlight. Well back under an overhang, Mike Morley and I crouch against the wall and against our sleeping bags, ready soon to sleep.

The shelter, one of the cubbyholes in the cliff face, feels like a cave. Our voices are boxed in, our heads turned down from the hard ceiling. Snow dusts our boots. The headlamp, feeble against the dark, intensifies the sense of isolation.

We are tucked irretrievably down here, buried a thousand times over by distance and topographic lines and mid-December weather. This is a northeast-trending canyon where the Kaibab formation offers honeycombs of ledges and alcoves. No recorded route connects the top and bottom of this canyon, so we brought more than 300 feet of rope and miscellany to help get us somewhere. Maybe not all the way to the river, but somewhere. We turn off the headlamp, and the canyon goes black. Even after a long silence, I know all eyes are open. We may as well be in space.

We had started this walk earlier today by slinging our packs out of the truck and into a snowstorm. Cattle

MINERS OR EXPLORERS DEVELOPED ALL OF THE MAIN HUMAN TRAILS IN THE GRAND CANYON BY FOLLOWING PREHISTORIC ROUTES. THE PREHISTORIC PEOPLE, OF COURSE, WERE FOLLOWING THE NATURAL BREAKS IN THE LANDSCAPE, THE FAULTS AND FISSURES THAT ALLOWED THEM ACCESS INTO THE CANYONS. THESE WERE ROUTES THE BIGHORN SHEEP USED BEFORE ANY HUMAN WALKED HERE.

Opposite: Near Boulder Narrows, a backpacker follows the course of the Colorado River toward North Canyon, which joins the Colorado River a half mile above River Mile 21.

country. Stock tanks. Saltbrush and big sage. This is the northeastern reach of the Grand Canyon where the river cuts a dagger called Marble Canyon. There are fewer tributary canyons here, but each one is precise and deep into the landscape like knife cuts. This skeletal geometry is unlike the rest of the Grand Canyon. Across the top it could be mistaken for a broad, featureless basin, the canyons concealed. You might believe you could walk unhindered 15 miles from the Vermilion Cliffs to the Echo Cliffs, as if it were an east Kansas plain. But a couple miles along this walk, the ground suddenly will open. Range horses at full gallop have sailed off the edge.

THE GROUND FROZE LAST NIGHT and, under a clear morning sky, we travel on sand as hard as rock. On the floor of this canyon we descend into the planet. Kaibab, Toroweap, Coconino, Supai. To advance, we must renegotiate each of our moves at every fallen boulder. A contract made with a handhold upcanyon will not be valid at the next rock. Weight will be thrown in a slightly different direction, left hand used to brace instead of a shoulder, thumb and forefinger on a small block or a single finger in a notch to hold — for half a second — the entire weight of the body.

I have been with Mike for more than 20 days in the wilderness now.

I have watched him. Not like a voyeur, but like watching an animal work among river cobbles. His voice has become softer, his choice of gestures more delicate. He has cultivated a certain way of stepping on a rock, finding its center, moving across it so as not to steal its stability with his boot. Now he moves down the canyon like water.

When we find things, we stop. A root that has coiled into a particular shape. The print of a bighorn sheep moving across the canyon rather than along the bed. New stones lie in the wash — small black stones and pieces of petrified wood — revealing a higher web of drainages. For the majority of the Grand Canyon, the uppermost rock is the Kaibab formation. Here, the canyons stretch into formations to the north and west, where pieces of Navajo and Moenkopi formations have been captured and dragged downstream. After months of walking other canyons in the park, all of them collecting the same stones in their beds, I see these new colors stand out like stabs of sunlight. In the hand, they feel unusual. The novelty of these weights, textures, and colors pleases me. I feel as if I now understand something that months ago I did not.

As we walk, the hard Supai formation alters the canyon's frame. The

floor becomes devoid of boulders, a phenomenon often apparent as a main channel forms in bedrock and prepares to dive. The compressing funnel of flood water discriminates less in narrow places, removing sand and boulders with equal speed. Here, erosion is more advanced.

Our movements slow, becoming detailed as we pick certain routes and shuffle across catwalks. Then, out of a keyhole in the canyon floor, comes a 50-foot free-fall. We walk to the edge where a pool of water hangs. The only place to stand is on a thin, rounded lip. Looking off the edge, I tell Mike that I am worried. How many more of these will there be? I talk about luck and hope, but we both know these are lies. There is no luck or hope in here. Only a canyon.

We anchor a rope to boulders. Mike rappels first, weighted with his pack. As he passes the lip, he is gone, so I watch tight reverberations in the rope. I can't see him from here. His voice sounds strained. Loose flakes, he says. Don't grab them, they'll come loose. A deep overhang. Difficult to keep balance.

"Oh, my God," he says. "It's fantastic in here."

I stand in this sandstone vestibule, its conical walls around my body. It is the narrowest space so far in the drainage, a place where floods go mad. I run my hands over the scallops. Mike yells that he's down and off the rope. I remain with my hands on the rock for a few more seconds, looking for clues. Clues to the passage of water, to the shape of stone. I rig my harness into the rope and step off the edge. The rope tightens against my weight. I rappel down through a curved interior dome, a

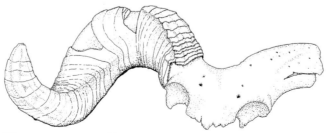

The broken skull of a bighorn ram, left horn missing.

place where echoes get trapped, as they do in the high vaults of a cathedral. Near the bottom, I run out of grace, nearly tipping backwards with the weight of my pack. Boots touch down. I come to my knees to steady the weight of my pack. I look around before releasing the rope. We've passed into farther country.

WE WONDER OUT LOUD IF ANYONE has been here before. Probably. Probably not. There is no way of knowing. It shouldn't be different down here; it is the same canyon, but the air is changed. Our voices echo with an intangibly altered quality. A collapsed section of canyon wall lies like a spilled armload of books. The rope dangles before us, as if we'd come down from the ceiling of a mosque. It is scandalous that we have arrived in here. We leave the rope behind in case we must return and use it as an escape route.

The next obstacle is a pool of water, a bowl too deep to skirt, squeezed tight between walls. We strip naked with little discussion. It is best not to talk, not to think at the edge of water this time of the year. Insulation of overhanging walls has kept it from freezing. I leap in, up to my chest, turn around to grab my pack. Air presses out of my throat, making a desperate sound. I bite my lip, carry the pack on my head. When I come out the other side — my body painted bright green with algae — I look and smell like a salad. We do not bother to dry off. Just get dressed and keep moving, before the shivering maddens us. My feet are hard from the cold. My boots feel as if they are filled with razor blades.

Eventually, the canyon leads to the river. When we get that far, to the canyon's conclusion, we separate and find polished boulders where we stand almost inside of the rapids. The rapids sound startlingly loud, like an accident, something being torn to pieces and never stopping. I did not think we would make it here by nightfall. The vagaries of these canyons amaze me. How one will be impossible to follow and another will allow us passage with only a rappel and a swim. How one will give us sand floors and another will offer boulders the size of houses. How we squeeze in through a crack in the door and now are in a distant land.

We sleep beneath a south-facing ledge and wake long before the sun reaches us. We discuss the next leg of the route. Travel along the river. Upstream. I have heard of a route along the river, but I have no details. So we start upstream through a clutter of collapsed walls. Marble Canyon is fresh with erosion. The clean, new rifts lay jams of boulders all over. Where rockslides have built eddies in the river below, hook-jawed rainbow trout swim.

The canyon pinches against the water, and Mike tests the area ahead. First, he wades into the river, then he climbs the wall. He clutches an overhanging block, his body tangled in water reflections and in strands of black widow webs. He says that it is no good, there is no way up. We backtrack a mile, scramble to a narrow bench of sandstone 400 feet above the river, and start out again.

NOW WE FIND THE SIGNS of bighorn sheep — cloven prints; small, hard acorn scat that turns black and cracked over the months;

bunch grass chewed down, but not all the way to the nub. Bighorns tear the grass blades rather than cleanly cut them because the sheep lack upper incisors. We've looked for these areas, where the bighorn have walked. Bighorn know how to travel here. They rarely dabble in dead ends. We are borrowing from their greater familiarity with this terrain.

You can't walk a straight line out here. You will always backtrack or gain elevation when your eventual goal is descent. This is not like navigating across an ocean. This place is a thousand horizons interrupting each other as you look farther and farther. Knowledge of maps, magnetic directions, or distances isn't the answer. If you tried to walk straight ahead, you would be confounded within a few steps, trapped by palisades. The route that must be taken depends on the lay of certain boulders and an archway behind a fallen Supai wall. A line of complex, suggestive landmarks. Places that look like routes, but do not bear the signs of bighorns, often end in sudden drops. Whenever we lose their tracks, we find that we must turn back.

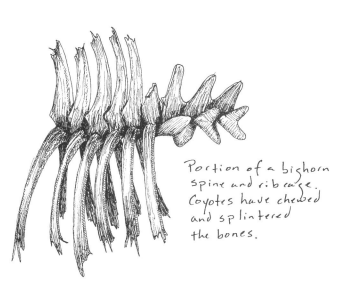

Portion of a bighorn spine and ribcage. Coyotes have chewed and splintered the bones.

Above: A backpacker follows a trail along a barren, rocky ledge pioneered by bighorn sheep near River Mile 160. Some of the creatures he may encounter down in the Canyon include, from left, a pink rattlesnake, a horned toad, and a collared lizard.

Following
An Obscure Route

WILD AND CAPTIVE BIGHORNS have shown a keen memory of people, even a recollection of certain clothing. Their knowledge of the land they walk, to the smallest details of boulders, undoubtedly aids their dexterity. Indigo buntings will fly in reference to star patterns. Waterfleas orient toward certain vectors of polarized light. Humans often use gridded maps. The desert bighorn sheep navigate by space and landmarks and memory. Theirs is perhaps the most original and accurate sense of place. Even considering their notoriously bad night vision, I have listened to them maneuver difficult Redwall ledges on moonless nights. On these night walks, they kick more rocks than during the day. Still, they recalled the course step by step and followed it safely to the bottom of the canyon.

Miners or explorers developed all of the main human trails in the Grand Canyon by following prehistoric routes. The prehistoric people, of course, were following the natural breaks in the landscape, the faults and fissures that allowed them access into the canyons. These were routes the bighorn sheep used before any human walked here.

I spoke with an archaeologist about this once. Helen Fairley had worked for eight years in the park. "Along come the backpackers today," she said. "Over and over and over again, you would see them gravitating to the very same places that prehistoric people had lived in. Because of the constraints of the landscape, the constraints of water, the views — just this inherent, innate programming as human beings to be drawn to specific places that are conducive to living. It doesn't really matter if you're Havasupai or an Archaic hunter and gatherer. For travelers in the Canyon, there are certain

necessities that cause us to gravitate to certain places."

The tracks of bighorn sheep simplify the process, as we trail behind their adroitly cataloged sensitivity to this confusing landscape.

We walk ahead to ledges so narrow that we tap with our boots to knock off the small, ball-bearing pebbles that threaten a good step. We wait for the rocks to stop falling, curious to see how far they will go — 20, 60 feet — before we walk further. Eventually, we are brought back to the river, where we slog through loose, quartz-rich sand, then climb again. By dark we reach the next side canyon. We set a simple camp at House Rock Rapids, staying up long enough to watch the high walls turn to white clay in the moonlight. At one point, the light takes all of the canyon except the floor, leaving the rapids to snap in the dark.

IN THE MORNING, BACK ON A bighorn route, we follow the scattering of dark pellets up a canyon and away from the river. The place is classic Marble Canyon, narrow and solitary, like a single chisel stroke. It is an artwork of rock layers, each eroding to a different cadence, stacking like dishes. I lie on my stomach and wedge the tip of my boot, locking hands with Mike to pull him up. At the next small rim he turns and does the same for me.

Too often a person traveling on trails expects that there will always be a route, that rocks will erode into steps, that the ledge will not sand down to a cliff. Instead, I find that the canyon shapes have nothing to do with my stride or the reach of my arm. So my

way of moving changes. I try to think of bighorn decisions: to go up or down, the ladder-rung cracks or a jump to a lower level, the fat boulders or the thousand smaller rocks that spill around my boots.

A BIGHORN RAM APPEARS. MIKE sees him first. Then a ewe behind him. They watch us, leap through boulders outlining the slope of Hermit shale, then stop to watch again. Their motions are as true and confident as chess moves. The ewe leaps eight vertical feet to take a ledge. They hesitate only before jumping upward, when they shrink their necks, coiling back their center of gravity to make it easier to fly. We hold still. A wind rakes up the canyon. It chills the backs of our ears, slaps us with the ends of our backpack straps. The sheep take perches to observe us, landing on boulder tops, then waiting a few seconds before turning to look in our direction. The pause almost implies nonchalance. They do not choose hiding places. They take good views, posing themselves clearly.

At a run, they follow each other in a jump to the floor, clearing 15 feet, their bodies shocking down upon impact. The energy of the impact springs into the next step, which they use to cross the canyon floor in less than a second. When they are gone, we walk to this place. We consider the jumping distance, the force of the landing. Mike steps off a much shorter drop to test his knees.

Three months ago, I got a close look at a bighorn ram at the junction of Willow Canyon and Tuckup Canyon, far west of here, where the upper portions of Redwall limestone are smooth and colored a soft blue. I sat in the shade, surrounded by wavy cloak ferns (found growing only in limestone). The ram appeared 50 feet across from me in full daylight. He stood close enough that I could study the cowlick in his hairs, wound just behind the front leg over his ribs. Rings ran wave-like down the horns. He angled his head slightly, like a dog hearing an odd pitch. He knew I was there. He placed his hooves silently and in a very particular manner, setting them down so lightly as to barely dust the rock with his weight.

I seemed to be causing some consternation, because he began pacing. Then, abruptly, he sat down on a ledge of prickly pear cactus. His eyes narrowed contentedly. Once before, I had seen a ram sit down like this in my presence. I can't tell you what the action means. It seemed to be a way of saying that the intruder was of little consequence.

Desert bighorn, generally the largest mammals in this part of the desert and which tend to stand on rocks where they can be seen, are well-studied, but we've learned only so much. They flee into the rocks to avoid close observation. Their stories of small errors are told in bones left across the desert.

It is difficult to know enough about such animals, and we understand little even of what we've seen, such as their clear physical characteristics. A variety of desert bighorn sheep have pink tongues, which is somehow associated with animals of wide, spreading horns, deep chests, and thin flanks. Notably wary of humans, animals of this variety scatter if people come within a mile. Another genetic strain, those with purely black tongues, are far less skittish. They often allow people to approach slowly or, perhaps out of curiosity, they walk toward visitors, even in remote areas

where they would tend to be most wild. Black-tongued bighorns have tight, curling horns and robust, blocky bodies. We don't know clear reasons for these physical associations, but we know that black tongues, because of their curiosity or ease with humans, are most often killed by hunters. The rest is guesswork.

AFTER SOME TIME, THIS RAM stood from his cactus bed. He snapped up a mouthful of broom snakeweed — flowers, stems, and all. For half an hour he jawed this one bite, chewing counterclockwise, keeping post on me. I made few movements, trying not to startle him. I could see his boyish tuft of tan, unkempt hair between the horns. There is a dramatic certainty to a bighorn sheep in the desert. Compared to the remainder of the Colorado Plateau, I've noticed an extraordinary lack of wildlife within the Grand Canyon. People attribute this to the intensity of the landscape, to the chore of getting from one place to the next,

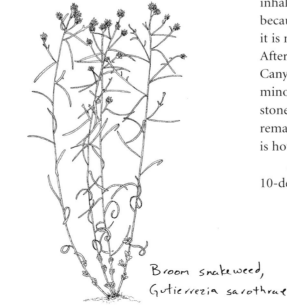

Broom snakeweed,
Gutierrezia sarothrae

leaving certain canyons like barely inhabited islands. But still there are bighorns.

When he finally walked away, the last thing I saw was the white stripe of hairs down the axis of his hind legs. I stood and climbed out of the shade into the sharp, early September sun. At the bottom of the canyon, I filled my bottle with pooled flood water, then slapped a handful on my forehead.

DECEMBER'S WATER NOW IS difficult to find. The full basins are frozen solid. The season has changed completely into winter. At night, we walk in moonlight with our packs, water in our bottles freezing faster than we can drink. I remember that months ago, back when I watched the bighorn, I spent my time seeking a certain quality of shade, morning shade that flowed like a delicacy until the sun shooed it away. I had been appalled at how that ram had just stood there in afternoon sunlight that, on my skin, felt like furnace heat. Now the cold is everything. Inside of my sleeping bag and my bones. Inside the rocks. Barely tagged with cirrus, the sky inhales the cold. We walk in the night because December days are so short and it is more comfortable than being still. After four months of walking the Grand Canyon, I feel embedded here, like some minor flaw in the rock, an off-colored stone along the floor. Something that remains through the seasons, whose skin is hot in summer, frigid in winter.

After sunrise, trying to stretch the 10-degree night from my boots, I walk back to the top of the canyon we had descended days ago. We've made a circle now, returning to where — days ago — we had left my truck in a snow storm. I am walking back into this canyon to finish my business here, to close the circle. Mike remains at camp for the day as I enter the shade and travel across frozen mud and the backs of boulders.

Inside, I find a place cleared of vegetation where a bighorn ram had died. The skeleton is complete, unfolded in a small embayment as if each bone had been arranged in ceremony. I slip out of my pack and kneel before the skull. The horns are in full curl, grown so far around and forward that the animal hardly could have avoided staring at them. They are butterscotch-colored against the eggshell white of bones. I touch them. They are hard and chipped. My hand barely grips half the circumference of one horn. I lift it. Fifteen, 20 pounds, I would say. Then I stand, holding this bulky, bow-shaped sculpture before my chest.

I think briefly about stealing it. I want it to be mine, a belonging that will tell of where I have been. It is sometimes hard to shake the wish to own. I feel less concerned about federal or Park Service regulations governing such matters than I do about other, less revisable laws. Indeed, the skull does not belong to the government or to the American people. It does not belong to me. It is an object of the canyon and of itself. It is testimony to a long-lived animal (perhaps 10 or 12 years) that held intimate knowledge of this region. Its memory was a map of routes around Marble Canyon. Now it is a spread of bones. I finally lower the skull so the horns rest back in their grooves in the soil.

The site apparently was carefully chosen. It has a view to quick escape

routes, but boulders conceal it on several sides. A mountain lion could have dragged the ram here, but for reasons difficult to explain, I believe that it arrived on its own. The tough fibrous material of horns and hooves will outlast all of these bones by a number of years.

The horns read like a story. Most of the lengthy horn growth occurs in the first few years, pushed by sex hormones that leave deep annular rings. After that, the pronounced curl begins and the horn bases become bulky, widening until they overwhelm the skull. Much like the rings of a tree, horn rings keep track of major changes. These rough corrugations itemize hormonal surges, seasonal changes, and times of little water or excessive food. The most recent rings grew closest to the head, pushing the earliest ones out toward the ends, which are splintered like brooms. The frayed tips record the ram's physical motions, how the animal moved through brush or dragged its horns against the rock of narrow passageways.

Much like the eroded shapes of canyons, the horns are archives, etched with each event and passing. This entire place is a chronicle of rock and bone, the shape of a bighorn curl as acutely formed as the curve of a canyon wall.

I have a long walk today, reaching a certain point, then returning by night. I had promised myself that I would not stop for long at anything. But I can't help it here. Crouched in front of these bones, I have no wish to move. The ram's pelvis is surprisingly small. The air is chilled. The boulders are Coconino fallen across slopes of Hermit shale.

Pieces of stories everywhere. Book pages torn out and thrown into the wind. I climb out of the boulders around the skeleton and return to the dry bed.

SIX MILES DOWN, I REACH THE climbing rope we left slung over the lip. Earlier, we had debated whether it would be worth the day's effort to hike back down this canyon to retrieve our gear. The nature of a rappel in a place like this is that the anchor up top is abandoned once you reach the canyon below. Eventually, floods would erase our anchor, twisting the brightly colored webbing, abrading it to nothing. We reasoned that few if any people would ever find the evidence. There had been no footprints or charcoal in the canyon above, no cairn, no clearing where someone had scratched out a place to sleep. No one.

So we decided to return and gather these last pieces. This act is not to soothe our minds or to clean the land for other travelers. It is the closing of this circle. We will leave the canyon unaltered, slipping out with our shadows. Removing this equipment is perhaps an inconsequential act. If nothing else, it voices a wish for the Grand Canyon to remain an empire without our colored ropes and redundant footprints. It is a place where time will reduce a bighorn skeleton to powder without interruption. Where humans are careful with their steps. That is why we came in the first place.

I pull the rope and work out the knots. The canyon closes as I do this. It slips out of my hands, out of my reach. One turn to glance downcanyon. Then, the rope is coiled, and I am gone. Winter continues without pause.

VULCAN'S REALM

NEAR RIVER MILE 159, TWO SLENDER, VOLCANIC DIKES UNPRETENTIOUSLY
SLICE DOWN A WALL, CROSS THE RIVER, AND RISE UP THE OPPOSING CLIFF.

The dikes seem misplaced and mystifying until, 20 miles downstream, all hell breaks loose. There, at Mile 178, a careless boater devoted to a mid-channel route would collide with Vulcan's Anvil, a volcanic neck, the core of a volcano. This is the introduction to Vulcan's Realm.

Vulcan's Realm possesses a well-defined gateway just downstream from the Anvil. To enter Vulcan's Realm, you must be baptized by the most violent of rapids in the Grand Canyon. You now enter the beginning of a 10-mile segment literally plastered with the frozen cascades of lava.

Vulcan's Realm is lower and hotter than the upper Grand Canyon. The transition from Sonoran to Mojave Desert is already behind you. Now, teddy bear cholla gather on the benches, ocotillos wave from the ledges, and creosote bush disperse across exposed slopes.

The lava cascades (where the molten rock poured down the cliffs of the Grand Canyon) commence near Lava Falls and the Toroweap Fault. They end at Hurricane Fault in the vicinity of Whitmore Wash. But the lava flows (where the molten rock meandered down the Canyon along the bed of the Colorado) continue for over 80 miles more. Today, only remnants of the lava flows remain, but their patterns of columnar jointing and tumbled boulders continue to dominate.

Evidence is scant, but indications exist that at least some of at least 100 lava flows created natural dams that stoppered the Colorado, forming huge lakes above the obstruction and, for a time, depriving the Canyon downstream of a flowing river. Scenes of such stupendous destruction in the Canyon have never been witnessed by human beings, but Powell envisioned it: "What a conflict of water and fire there must have been here! Just imagine a river of molten rock running down into a river of melted snow. What a seething and boiling of the waters; what clouds of steam rolled into the heavens!"

Much more recently and farther downstream, a man-made dam has held back the Colorado, flooding the western-most regions of the Grand Canyon. Hoover Dam backs Lake Mead all the way to near Mile 240. For 40 more miles, river runners travel on a lake rather than a living, swirling, pulsing river. And there, at Mile 277, the faithful Kaibab limestone suddenly crashes downwards into the low desert along the Grand Wash Cliffs — and the Grand Canyon abruptly, and convincingly, ends.

Opposite: Slabs of Supai sandstone test fate at Toroweap Overlook while the Colorado River growls with impatience 3,000 feet below. Toroweap lies on the Esplanade, a broad, 160-mile long bench situated 1,000 feet below the Rim.

[111]

The Colorado River and the Grand Canyon change moods constantly.

Changing Temperaments

Opposite: The violence of Lava Falls Rapids just below River Mile 179 distorts perceptions of time and space. Nearly all sources record its drop as 37 feet, while surveyors insist it measures only a little more than 14 feet.

Left: In the afternoon sun, the Colorado River glitters contentedly after a wild descent through Lava Falls Rapids, while a piñon pine watches stoically from the edge of the Esplanade in a shrubland setting.

Above: Downstream, the river continues in a milder mood under the guard of a desert plant, an ocotillo.

Opposite and above: These slopes consist of Tapeats sandstone sprinkled with teddy bear cholla. In the Grand Canyon, teddy bear cholla grows only downstream from Lava Falls. Diamond Peak looms in the distance in the photo at left.

Cholla Forest

Above: Just beyond the cholla forest, limestone terraces rise thousands of feet from river level in the western Grand Canyon near River Mile 223.

A Terraced Wall

Above: Travertine Canyon and its waters join the Colorado on its south side at River Mile 229.

Finding the Way

Opposite: Water in the Grand Canyon always finds the way to the Colorado River. Here, like a living symphony, the water cascades from the shaded confines of Travertine Grotto.

Above: The Colorado River reluctantly
Calming Waters   turns into
Lake Mead.

Opposite: At this point, River Mile 239, Separation Fault
History and   crosses the Colorado River. At Separation
Geology   Canyon in 1869, three members of Major
John Wesley Powell's group of explorers
left the expedition and soon were killed.

Above: Floating algae mats and spiky cattails enliven

Lake Mead Invades

Spencer Creek near River Mile 246.

Opposite: The Grand Canyon abruptly ends where the Colorado River leaves the Colorado Plateau at Grand Wash Cliffs, River Mile 277, and pools into Lake Mead behind Hoover Dam.

A WINTER'S
WALK

THE SEASON CHANGE CAME THE SECOND WEEK IN OCTOBER.
SUMMER ENDED AS IF A CORD HAD BEEN PULLED. I HAD WALKED TO A
smooth deck of Esplanade sandstone, near the South Bass Trail, and set a camp near the edge. Sitting there barefoot, I looked up, and summer was over. Damndest thing. This is how it happens every year. In a matter of days, the sun drops and its light turns low and angular, yawning over the canyons. Shade has a vivid autumnal coolness.

There is a different way of sleeping when fall arrives. It is described in my journal, October 12:

"For the last month my world has consisted of naked sleeping, and days of cautiously stepping through narrow canyons. Now the air is sharp. I feel good. My belongings are on the rock to my left. The chill is delicate, the first I've felt since last winter."

This change of season — it's like being handed a new life.

I SEE SOMEONE
WORKING HIS BOOTS THROUGH
THE SNOW. HEAD DOWN.
SHOULDERS HUMPED FORWARD.
HIS FACE LOOKS LIKE
A RESULT OF
A TRYING NIGHT.
DULL, VACANT EYES.
HE CAN'T HOLD
EYE CONTACT.
LATE 20S, MAYBE 30S.
"BE CAREFUL DOWN THERE,"
HE SAYS, WITH MORE
OF A GROAN THAN
AN ACTUAL VOICE,
"THAT CANYON ALMOST
KILLED ME."

WHAT I AM WITNESSING NOW IS
the full weight of winter. It is the second week of January. The passage from autumn to winter rarely has as sharp an edge as summer into autumn. The cold just sets in week after week, the same

Opposite: After a March blizzard, a backpacker finds that returning to the South Rim is a tedious but beautiful trek on the Bright Angel Trail.

way summer heat gathers over the weeks until you are carrying it on your back. Rocks down in the desert no longer hold the heat of sunlight. Snow buries the rims.

I am coming off the Rim on the South Kaibab Trail. It may be sunrise, but little light is getting through the storm. Fifteen feet of visibility. Winds burst out of the Canyon, assailing the Rim where I am setting the first tracks of morning. Snowdrift cornices sweep upward, coming to mid-calf, crawling up the walls of Kaibab formation where the wind scoops on itself.

I figured it best to use one of the large, maintained trails in this kind of weather. At its narrowest, the trail is several feet wide and hardened by millions of travelers and pack mules. The park officially documents 500 miles of trails. Trail crews maintain only 33 miles of that. But these groomed trails cannot overcome the topography of the Grand Canyon. The switchbacks aim down like a spiral staircase.

This is one of those demanding storms. It drives snow into my ears and switches its winds from side to side as if scrambling for a foothold. The heaviest part probably is over the North Rim right now. There, without snowshoes, I'd be up to my armpits in snowdrifts.

It is a different kind of forest on that Rim — a different world. Stands of ponderosa pine, spruce, and fir dominate the North Rim, which slopes upward to more than 9,000 feet. In these thickets, the heavily branched trees may clutter the view. The 7,000-foot-high South Rim supports mostly well-spaced ponderosa pines, the ground usually dry to the touch and carpeted with pine

needles and oak leaves. On the North Rim, the earth has a bit of mulch, where summer's *Amanita* mushrooms poke up through fallen aspen leaves. The elevation difference is enough to matter: The South Rim gets 26 inches of precipitation a year, while the North Rim has 40 inches. The canyon floor gets about eight inches a year.

Even considering the great differences in elevation and precipitation, the mean low temperatures on both rims may vary by only three degrees. It tends to be about 18° F. here. The North Rim acts like a south-facing window, bringing in sunlight. Coming down from the North Rim forests and onto the exposed canyon walls, you will notice sunlight's direct impact. There is less shade on the north side. Snow melts quickly under clear skies as the heat draws moisture from the soil. Vegetation becomes sparse, compared to that in the sheltered canyons under the South Rim.

Look at some of the spires and temples inside the Grand Canyon. The South Rim's north-facing slopes grow thick with junipers and piñons, while the North Rim has mostly rock and some scrubby purple sage. The northern slopes in steady sunlight tend to be

about 20 degrees warmer than those on the south side of the canyon.

Walking down from the dry South Rim, you will come across window-box habitats, niches of coolness where lush gardens grow. The top of the South Rim itself lacks the Douglas fir stands common to the North Rim. But in these enclaves below the South Rim, Douglas firs crouch against each other like children playing hide-and-seek, protected from the sun. I've seen healthy ponderosa pines as low as 3,500 feet, which is a flat-out desert elevation. They're tucked under ledges of Tapeats sandstone, on the south side. Stand in one of these window boxes and look across. The other side of the Grand Canyon will appear mostly bare.

RIGHT NOW, I CAN'T SEE MUCH. The trail looks as if it hangs from wires over a gray and endless space. Walking down through Coconino sandstone, I am looking to my left off the edge, which drops abruptly into nothing. I have to turn my boots sideways on the ice, under the snow, so I can find purchase with the edge of my soles. It is

Four narrowleaf yuccas on the dry, exposed slopes below the North Rim, Yucca angustissima.

a cold snow, fine and dusty, lacking the doily snowflake edges you would get if it were just five or 10 degrees warmer. It whips around easily on the wind.

On December 12, 1931, Edwin McKee, who was living at the South Rim, recorded 18 inches of snow for the day. "Early this fall," he wrote, "the Supai Indians were very busy gathering piñon nuts. They said there was a long, cold winter ahead. When I asked how they knew, I was told that the abundance of the nut crop gave certain evidence. Even though the weather forecasting of the Supais is not based on modern scientific methods, it seems to have been accurate at least on this occasion. The winter has definitely started out as a long, cold one."

This year, the first substantial snowfall arrived at the South Rim the fourth week of October; three inches overnight. The next day, it was melted by noon. It has turned out to be a common winter: Sunlight ravaging the snow, then storms socking into canyons, spurs of clouds roaming around the inner gorges — lost for days after the storms have gone — warm afternoons on the Tonto Platform, shadows long, and rainstorms lumbering into the desert.

Regardless of what larger air masses pass over the Grand Canyon, interior canyons harbor mostly deviant local winds. Because the North and South Rims are heating at vastly different rates, daytime winds drop off the south and rise up the north. In the evening, both rims radiate warmth, sending breezes toward the river. Between day and night, north and south, and the various individual canyons, a sloshing effect is created inside the Grand Canyon.

Imagine a tub of water being rocked back and forth, only this is a tub of air, rocked by differential heating. A test station set on the south side found that more than half of the Grand Canyon winds are either rising straight out of the canyons or falling into them.

Even with all of this swishing around, winds rarely transport air over the rims and out of the Canyon. The air that is down there, stays there. It is visible when pollution drops into the interior. The haze stirs evenly between canyons, but cannot escape. These vertical winds can be felt from low in the canyons, especially early on summer evenings, when threads of air trace the bottoms where water might run. You breathed this same air in the morning before it blew to the rim and came back.

In the mid-1930s, an assistant chief ranger named George Collins penned his observations of Canyon winds, which he called "wind rivers of the Grand Canyon." He noticed that the airplanes were lifted when they crossed over the Canyon during the heat of the day.

He wrote: "Apparently, the air rolls and twists in a continuous side play, attendant on the general trend. But in all the mysterious tumult of convection currents, which one would see if the air were visible, the great up-draft would no doubt be the most imposing feature. Just as a symphony is built around a central theme, so does our fountain 'carry the air' in the magnificent symphony of inner-canyon winds."

THE WINDS THIS MORNING ARE OF a different nature. They are winter storm winds, built of turbulence from a large system dragging itself over the Canyon. Vortices are set up behind cliff faces, great swirling eddies inscribed in the clouds. I stop at one of the long points of land under the Coconino. I've seen ravens here in better weather. I've sat on this point in the fall and watched them play the rising air, banking and swimming around one another. Now, I stop and look into the bottomless Canyon, wondering where ravens go. This peninsula of Hermit shale just hangs here. I feel as if I'm being held out for sacrifice and that the Grand Canyon is this gulping infinity beneath my feet. No sign of solid ground anywhere. Occasionally, I will see something, some tip of land suspended out there. Then it is gone.

Now I see the ravens. They rise out of the abyss, taking form where there should be nothing. Two of them look like black shreds of fabric hurled against the storm. They spin up, pausing over my head to take account of this figure standing in the clouds. This close, I can see the curve of their armored toes, tucked under as if holding a marble or a stone. (Damn ravens, coming here without parkas or backpacks or extra food. Swirling through this storm as if it were a playground.) I have to protect my eyes with a hand. The wind takes snow down my neck, against my skin. Once the ravens get a good look at me, they continue up and are absorbed. And I'm standing here alone.

I TURN BACK DOWN THE TRAIL. Within a couple of minutes, I see someone coming up. He moves slowly, working his boots through the snow. Head down. Shoulders humped forward.

He must have started walking from the desert during the night, or slept in the snow, which is not too uncomfortable if a person has the right gear and the proper mind set. As he approaches, I can see he looks like he's just been rolled from a dumpster. Plastic garbage bags cover his body. He's torn a hole in the bottom of one in order to breathe and see ahead. The clothes underneath are insufficient. Maybe he's got a sweater and coat. In both hands are walking sticks, their tops splintered, as if they were hastily broken for this purpose.

He doesn't notice me until I am about four feet away. When he sees my legs in the snow, he inches his head up a notch. His face looks like a result of a trying night. Dull, vacant eyes. He can't hold eye contact. Late 20s, maybe 30s. "Be careful down there," he says, with more of a groan than an actual voice.

Down there. As if he had just climbed out of a monster's stomach — the empty space that gave birth to the ravens. I ask if he needs help. In the same ponderous tone, with a touch of anger, he says, "That canyon almost killed me."

As he passes, I turn and ask again, offering food or water. He does not stop,

does not ask how far to the Rim. In fact, his pace has not altered at all. "I'll make it," he says. I look for a limp or some sign of injury. There seems to be nothing but fatigue. He's close enough to the top that he'll be out within an hour. Like the ravens, he is taken in by the storm above me. Is he delirious? Had he fallen? I imagine him sledding down, arms flailing, and catching a piñon trunk just at the edge of a chasm, snow spraying all around him. His comment about the Canyon made it sound as if it were malevolent down there, as if he had narrowly escaped, and the Canyon still had his hair in its teeth.

So I FOLLOW HIS TRACKS. THEY keep to the trail down to Cedar Ridge, a clearing of hitching posts for mules and three outhouses. The outhouses are sturdy structures with a deck and solid wooden doors. His tracks begin here. I open the middle door and am confronted with a nest. My first thought is that some large animal burrowed here. It looks like a mouse nest on a huge scale. Wood chips, used for the composting toilets, are a foot deep all over the floor. Food wrappers lie unfolded. A bag of bread. A candy bar. A flashlight is propped on the toilet paper dispenser. He had slept here, using the chips as insulation. A locked storage closet joins the back of one of the toilets. Its door hangs off its hinges, ripped from the wall. He had found the plastic bags and wood chips in there, as well as the broom handle he'd busted for walking sticks. A box of screws and various small tools he had examined and rejected.

I would later discover that he had hiked to Phantom Ranch, down at the river, with the intention of returning to the Rim that night. It was a day hike. Backpackers had tried to talk him into staying. He had refused, mentioning that he needed to catch a plane. He accepted their offerings of a flashlight, bread, and candy, setting off for the South Rim in the late afternoon. When he reached the only emergency phone on the trail — at some outhouses 2,000 feet below here — he was desperate. Night had come. A storm had set in, bringing rain and wind. He had no idea that it would turn to snow above him. He made a call to the ranger at Phantom Ranch, and he sounded panicked. He wasn't asking for anything, just wanted to hear a human voice, said he had to catch a plane. The ranger patched him through to someone closer, but in the transfer, he dropped the phone and continued up the Canyon. The phone dangled off the hook, draining its solar battery.

He arrived at Cedar Ridge in a blizzard. Ice had formed on his clothing and he probably was suffering from hypothermia. When he found these outhouses, he found plastic bags and wood chips, enough to keep him alive. If he had not reached Cedar Ridge, I probably would have come across his body below O'Neill Butte, curled in the mud in one of the sheltered alcoves. No one at the Canyon knew his name or ever saw him again. There are only a few trails with outhouses and emergency phones. He was lucky.

The Grand Canyon was not the thing that almost killed him, as he had said. The Canyon is here, with its winds and sunshine at random intervals. There is no pretense. The rocks do not bear ill will, nor will they offer to save you. The

Winter-bare stalks of Prince's plume flowers, *Stanleya pinnata.*

Winter's Grip

Above: As curtains of mist rise at Toroweap Overlook in early January, visitors become an audience with balcony seats in the "Grand Canyon Theater."

Left: There's little room for error on the Grandview Trail when layers of ice and snow reduce the clearances for bulky backpacks.

Veils and Billows

Right: Clouds play in the Canyon below the South Rim.

Below: A May storm drops an afternoon curtain of snow across from Yavapai Point.

personality of storms deal with updrafts, moisture content, and temperature, not with grudges or malice. A person must learn how to move inside of this place. Like the ravens. I close the door and continue into the Canyon.

Beneath O'Neill Butte, at the rim of the Redwall, snow turns to rain. The Supai mud on top of the Redwall is a sloppy red, spattering on my pants legs. Clothes start coming off, layer by layer. It no longer is freezing. In fact, it is above 35°. This is where the clouds end. They look like a smooth underbelly, one solid mass hovering midway down the Canyon. Below here, everything is visible, all the surrounding canyons, and towers poking into the cloud ceiling. But there is no direct sunlight. The green of Bright Angel shale stands out in this rich, wet light. It looks like the color of army fatigues before they've been washed.

The trail takes me to the river, where it must be 50°, and the rain has stopped. Water has simply evaporated into the greater atmosphere. Looking up, I see that the entire world is under the weight of this storm. I can hold my hands up flat to its underside. I am now in a cotton shirt, sleeves rolled. I cross the Colorado River at a black footbridge and stop in the middle. Water sweeps below, greenish but mostly clear this season. Following the water is a current of cold air. It is a coolness that will last well into the spring. The river in April is a checkerboard of temperatures and light breezes. Pockets of warm and cool air drift over the water during the change of seasons. Warm air will float off the sunlit rocks. Cold air is from the river. By July, all of the air will turn hot. But

for now, air over the river feels like the breath of an ice box.

Since I got out of the hard cold, and especially down at the Redwall where the snow ceased, scents have been rising out of the Canyon: wet plants — blackbrush, brittlebush, broom snakeweed, and catclaw acacia. The pungent smell of wet poreleaf bush is strongest near the Vishnu schist. And within 500 feet of the river, the slightly sweet scent of arrowweed comes up.

From Rim to river are five biotic communities in the Grand Canyon — Hudsonian, Canadian, Transition, Upper Sonoran, and Lower Sonoran — and each has a different scent in wet weather. Walking through these communities (starting up in the snow and reaching the river by mid-morning) is like walking from the Canadian Rockies to the state of Sonora, Mexico, in less than 10 miles. This explains why the garbage-bag man chose to walk out. He was in the desert when he decided to turn back. How could he have known he was walking into a Canadian blizzard? During the summer, at least between monsoon storms, the smells are more robust up top and meager in the lower zones — marking a time of dormancy in

Scars of black bear claws on an aspen trunk in a North Rim forest.

the desert and a time of activity in the forest. The opposite is true this time of year. Plants are frozen in place on the Rim, while an entirely different set of species thrives in the mild temperatures at the bottom.

Between these extremes, 1,771 separate species of plants have been documented inside the Grand Canyon, which is comparable to the species diversity of the more lush, mountainous parks such as Sequoia or Yosemite. Yet, looking into the Grand Canyon, you will see mostly rock. The plant life appears like nothing but an afterthought, sprinkled conservatively across the few places horizontal enough to support any life at all. The Canyon's miscellany of climates allows for such a flourish of species. Considering the sheer volume of land within the Grand Canyon and the difficulties of surveying each of these canyons, there probably is a fair number of species yet to be documented. The Grand Canyon was not even botanically surveyed until 1938, when botanists Elzada Clover and Lois Jotter journeyed down the river. What they found was a multi-storied tree house of environments. They cataloged the plants they had seen or discovered, then mentioned that the canyon walls furnished opportunities for careful study into miniature, isolated climates.

This morning I have walked through half-a-globe of climates and ecosystems to reach this river. These are places where a disoriented hiker can easily become trapped in heavy snows and places where each day of July exceeds 105°. It is an elaborate landscape, even when looking beyond the shapes of canyons that first catch the eye.

WRITTEN IN ROCK

IT NEVER FAILS. EACH TIME THAT I ARRIVE AT THE RIM OF THE GRAND CANYON, I'M TAKEN ABACK, REALIZING THAT MY RECENT EXPERIENCES away from the Canyon have dulled common sense, that the earth is not two dimensional, it's three.

Peering into the Grand Canyon reminds me of examining a bodily gash — a reminder that the surface is only a facade. There are bones, muscle, connective tissue, blood, and machinery of unknown purpose in there. It's the same with the Grand Canyon. The view brings curiosity and some alarm. What are those structures? How did they get there? Are they dangerous?

Down there in that hidden world below the Rim, there are numerous natural systems with laws and customs unfettered by human regulations. One is geologic.

I've seen pebbles and stones come hurtling down Canyon slopes and cliffs. Most such minute events are initiated by assorted lizards, bighorn sheep, and mischievous ravens.

Gravity alone can trigger larger events. I recall only one instance when an ample slab of rock smashed to smithereens within my sight, and that was nearly a mile away. I never saw the rock itself, only a puff of dust followed by a gunshot-like report.

Flash floods, however, have come rumbling through my camps a number of times. They are the mechanisms that haul the fallen pebbles and rubble to the Colorado River, which, until dams were built, transported them to the sea. One of these uninvited liquid monsters came visiting at night and very nearly carried off a friend. We never did find one of his hiking boots.

Imagine trying to piece together the geologic history of the Grand Canyon and the rock strata from which it was hewn by snooping around its innards. With a group of geologists, I've done so. I felt totally inadequate. We were ants swarming over the foundations of a ruined city looking for random crumbs of a story.

Gathering geologic clues demands slow, patient work. Interpreting the clues often is difficult. An army of geologists has spent more than a century gathering enough crumbs to reconstruct the geologic story of Grand Canyon. They succeeded in revealing the outline of the Canyon's history. But many details are elusive, and deep mysteries remain.

Especially interesting to today's geologists are the older rocks in the Grand Canyon, down deep, where relatively recent geologic events have distorted and confused the evidence. Those rocks were formed at a time when life was gaining momentum after a couple of million millennia of stagnation and the planet was beginning to show promise of becoming the habitat we know today.

Opposite: A ribbon of silver, the Colorado River meanders between hills of Dox sandstone in a view from Hilltop Ruin, River Mile 71. Time and erosion have peeled away layers of rock, exposing clues left eons ago.

ABOUT THIS PORTFOLIO

U<small>NDERSTANDING THE GEOLOGY OF</small> G<small>RAND</small> C<small>ANYON CAN BE A JOY, BUT COMING TO</small>
understand it can be a source of woe. Much of the problem rests in the confusing
multitude of rock layers and formations — Kaibab, Toroweap, Coconino, Hermit,
Esplanade . . . right down to Vishnu at the bottom. Not everyone wishes to get friendly
with such a diverse and unruly gang of wrinkled and slightly scary characters.

But held within each set of rocks is a record of a place and time that dwelt here long
before there was even a hint of the Grand Canyon. The beauty of the rocks and their
stories begin 1.84 billion years ago; they end with the abrupt creation of Grand Canyon
only a geologic yesterday — 5 or 6 million years ago.

In brief, here's what happened as recorded in the soaring escarpments of the Grand
Canyon, beginning at the bottom.

Ancient Island Arcs

Opposite: The scene — Upper Granite Gorge, River Mile 96, September morning. The geology — beginning about 1.84 billion years ago, the Elves Chasm gneiss was formed as a volcanic arc. Some 90 million years later, the Granite Gorge metamorphic suite, including the Vishnu schist, was deposited as volcanic material and the sediments of eroded volcanic material on and near island arcs. Then, after an additional 50 million years, these tectonic plates collided with the southern edge of North America (today's Wyoming) to form the basement of the Grand Canyon region.

Right: The scene — downstream from Crystal Rapids, River Mile 99, September afternoon. The geology — during the arc collisions about 1.7 billion years ago, thousands of feet of Vishnu schist, having been sutured onto the edge of the continent and metamorphosed while buried to depths of 10 miles or more, were uplifted and injected with a web of pink granite veins and dikes.

Creation and Destruction of Mighty Mountains

Left: The scene — prickly pear cactus reach out from a tilting garden at Ruby Rapids. The geology — these rocks of Vishnu schist once were in the core of island mountains, similar to present-day Philippines.

Above: The scene — Vishnu schist sculpted by whirlpool currents and swirling eddies wielding nothing more than grit and sand, River Mile 113. The geology — creation of the Vishnu schist mountains also initiated their ultimate demolition. Erosion, in a few hundred million years, reduced the mountains to a near-featureless plane.

The Grand Canyon Supergroup

Opposite: The scene — brittlebush blooms at the Ottoman Amphitheater in late April. The geology — beginning about 1.25 billion years ago, the eroded Vishnu schist landscape began to subside. Oceans and seas swept in and a new sequence of deposits began to bury the Vishnu.

Left: The scene — Dox sandstone, part of the Grand Canyon Supergroup, forms outcrops near River Mile 66. The geology — for half a billion years, layers of Supergroup sandstones, shales, and lavas accumulated and reached a thickness of nearly three miles.

Below: The scene — the head of Tanner Rapids. The geology — displacement along a fault has brought Cardenas basalt (at left) alongside the younger Dox sandstone. This system of faults created upthrown ranges and shallow ocean basins as the continent was stretched and bedrock was broken into a series of fault-bounded blocks.

Wasting of the Supergroup

Right: The scene — sculpted Vishnu schist near River Mile 128. The geology — like the Vishnu schist mountains before them, the Supergroup mountains also were washed away by time and erosion. About 200 million years of erosion swept away nearly all of the 15,000 feet of Supergroup rocks.

Below: The scene — detail of the Great Unconformity, Blacktail Canyon. The geology — the underlying Vishnu schist, unburdened by the younger Supergroup rocks, once again saw daylight.

Opposite: The scene — waterweed and Vishnu schist outcrop with Tapeats sandstone cliffs on the far shore near River Mile 127. The geology — about 500 million years ago, the landscape subsided still again, flooding and burying the Vishnu basement and surviving pockets of Supergroup once more.

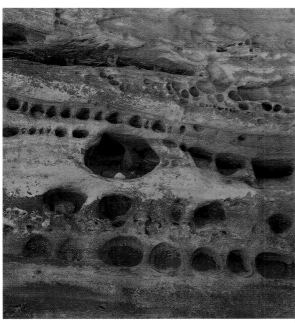

Tapeats Sandstone and The Great Unconformity

Opposite: The scene — Deer Creek free-falls past the Great Unconformity, River Mile 136. The geology — where the Supergroup is entirely missing, the Tapeats sandstone, first of the Paleozoic rocks, rests directly upon the Vishnu.

Left: The scene — detail of Tapeats sandstone, Blacktail Canyon. The geology — the Tapeats measures half a billion years in age, the underlying Vishnu about 1.7 billion. The Great Unconformity refers to the massive amount of time — about one-quarter of the history of the earth — left unrecorded along the boundary between the two strata.

Below: The scene — redbud tree in Deer Creek Narrows. The geology — the Tapeats walls are sculpted from course-grained sands laid down when the sea invaded the land. The Tapeats lies at the bottom of a thick sequence of rock layers accounting for three-quarters of the depth of today's Grand Canyon.

Opposite: The scene — near River Mile 55, ledges of

Bright Angel Shale

green and purple Bright Angel shale lie mantled in talus slopes. The geology — the Bright Angel shales, lying atop the Tapeats sandstone, are repositories of silt deposited near a continental margin and of diverse marine fossils that record an explosion in types of organisms on earth.

Above: The scene — in Awatubi Canyon. The geology — thin ledges of Bright Angel shale appear pink when illuminated by light reflected from a cliff and purple when illuminated by a clear blue sky.

Following panel: The scene — Muav limestone ledges on exhibit in

Muav Limestone

Matkatamiba Canyon, September afternoon. The geology — Muav limestone covered the Bright Angel shale as the Cambrian Ocean deepened and covered western North America.

Redwall Limestone

Opposite: The scene — near River Mile 23, April morning. Canyon explorer John Wesley Powell called the river-polished exposures of Redwall limestone the "Marble Pavement," a term later adopted in the naming of Marble Canyon. The geology — Redwall limestone was deposited in an ocean about 350 million years ago.

Right: The scene — Redwall limestone cliff towering over the Colorado River at River Mile 31. The geology — the Redwall is inherently gray but typically dresses in a cloak of red stains contributed by overlying strata.

Below: The scene — glowing limestone chamber in Jumpup Canyon. The geology — in some canyon sections, the Temple Butte limestone underlies the Redwall and the Surprise Canyon formation overlies the Redwall.

Supai Group

Following panel: The scene — a frog watches the photographer in North Canyon, early June morning. The geology — the Supai Group rocks are the evidence of streambeds, deltas, and estuaries of 300 million years ago.

Opposite: The scene — upstream from Soap Creek Rapids,
October morning. The geology — Hermit shale overlies the Supai ledges with bright red slopes. Ten Mile Rock, a dagger of Coconino sandstone fallen from the cliffs above, protrudes from the heart of the Colorado River.

Hermit Shale, Coconino Sandstone, and Toroweap Formation

Above: The scene — near Boysag Point on the North Rim. The geology — slopes of fiery red Hermit shale skirt sheer cliffs of creamy Coconino sandstone buttressing the ledgy cliffs and slope of overlying Toroweap formation. The Coconino is convincing evidence of coastal sand dunes, while the Toroweap tells of later subsidence and silty oceanic limestone deposition about 260 million years ago.

Kaibab Limestone Forms the Rim of the Grand Canyon

Above: The scene — a boulder of Kaibab limestone reviews its options near Buck Farm Point, late January. The geology — the Kaibab represents another episode of submergence and marine limestone deposition.

Opposite: The scene — the Colorado River near Lees Ferry, December afternoon. The geology — shortly after the deposition of the Kaibab limestone, an ecological catastrophe enveloped the earth. The nature of the event is unknown, but it brought an end to the Paleozoic Era, the time of "ancient life," as more than 80 percent of earth's species became extinct. At the future site of Grand Canyon, softer strata, such as the chocolate-hued Moenkopi formation, came to rest on and over the Kaibab limestone, assuring that a quarter billion years later the rim of the future Grand Canyon would stand conspicuous and distinguished.

The Creation of the Grand Canyon

Compared to the vast pageant of landscapes that preceded the present day, the Grand Canyon, geologically, is hardly more than a footnote — except it is ours, now, and seemingly forever.

The carving of the Canyon remains somewhat of a mystery. We know it happened recently, in only the last 5 or 6 million years. We know the Colorado River cut the Canyon (about a thousand cubic miles) and hauled away a still greater volume of rock that once lay above its present rim. We know the Canyon's birth was probably linked to the creation of the Gulf of California making possible a steep shortcut to the Pacific. But we can't seem to visualize the earliest stages of Canyon creation when the Colorado River most likely exited the incipient Grand Canyon via a lost valley. Was it to the northwest? Geologists continue the search for the final important details.

Right: Rays of sunlight slant toward Mount Hayden and the seemingly timeless Grand Canyon. The view is from Point Imperial on the North Rim.

WOODEN BOATS

LIKE A NEEDLE, THE COLORADO RIVER SEWS THE GRAND CANYON
TO THE PLANET. THE STITCHING STARTS BELOW LEES FERRY, IN A NARROW
chamber in the rock. Here, the Grand
Canyon first says its name out loud.
Here, its cliffs first reach enormous
height and breadth. Water hisses and
rumbles. The sound comes from the
rising and receding swells that
coil off the walls and boulders.
The first heavy shadows
appear. In the calmest
stretches, the water chases
its own tail, boiling, bunching
up, turning out spirals.

There is a dory down
here, a small wooden boat
that sways across these
spirals. It tends easily
to the side as its bow touches
an eddy. The dory's curved
bow, stern, and gunwales,
the flare of side walls, make it
look like a cello or a bass. Its
hull is made of marine plywood
strengthened with polished
fiberglass. Its gunwales and
oars are constructed of ash, its
oarlocks of brass, the bowpost of
Port Orford cedar. It was built in
the 1970s, named *Hidden Passage*
after a canyon that was consumed by
the reservoir of Glen Canyon Dam, just
upstream of here. It was built to run the
Colorado River.

Like the pink rattlesnakes and the
twining snapdragons, the rowers of these
dories are one of the Canyon's species.
They are the recipients of the river's
profusion and scarcity, taking account of

TO GIVE YOU EVEN
AN IDEA OF
THIS RIVER TRIP,
I WOULD HAVE TO
RUB SAND INTO
YOUR SCALP,
DRAG A ROCK ACROSS
YOUR FINGERTIPS
UNTIL THEY BLEED,
BURY YOU
IN MAIDENHAIR FERNS,
AND OFFER YOU
A PLACE TO SIT
IN THE EVENING
WHERE THE RIVER
WATER CURLS AT
YOUR BARE FEET.

Opposite: Jan Kempster battles the mad currents and angry
hydraulics of Lava Falls Rapids near River Mile 179.

changing water levels, watching light shift across seasons the way one day's sunlight moves over the land.

Elena Kirschner is on the oars. She's been guiding for Grand Canyon Dories for 14 years, since back when Martin Litton owned the business. With a 10-foot oar in each hand, she works the dory and the water with sweeping grace. Oars move forward in unison, dipping into the river, drawing back. Her movements are sparing, sensual, certain.

A passenger riding in the bow asks if he can hang the bailing scoop off the outside of the boat, so it won't rub against his knees. Elena hesitates.

"It wouldn't look as nice that way," she says.

The scoop stays in. It is not that anyone else would be displeased with the visual asymmetry of its being out (the other dories are too far away for anyone to notice). It is that this is a fine boat with which to grace the Canyon, and nothing should be out of place. We are here to experience beauty.

The trip will take about three weeks, covering 278 miles from the beginning of the Grand Canyon to the exit at Grand Wash Cliffs. I cannot tell you about this entire river — the details of each rapid, the side canyons it passes without anyone really seeing them. (In a day of travel on the river, you might glimpse 50 canyons and set foot in one or two). To give you even an idea of this river trip, I would have to rub sand

into your scalp, drag a rock across your fingertips until they bleed, bury you in maidenhair ferns, and offer you a place to sit in the evening where the river water curls at your bare feet.

I can tell you that sometimes, in these shadows and in the echoes of gulping water, I have the feeling that we are trespassing down here — lurking on the canyon floor like thieves.

The walls rise higher. Elena takes another draw on the oars, causing the water to sigh.

In 1869, ALL OF THE BOATS WERE made of wood. They had pronounced keels and V-shaped hulls, design flaws that made for difficult runs in the Canyon. That year, Major John Wesley Powell brought these cumbersome boats down to the river, assuming he could use a craft styled for the Mississippi River on these, then-uncharted, waters.

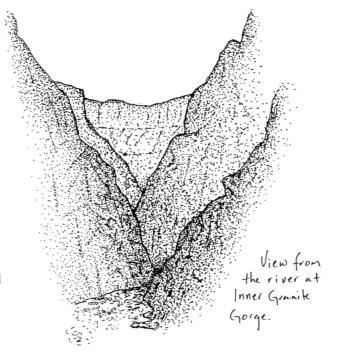

View from the river at Inner Granite Gorge.

P.T. Reilly, who operated wooden boats here in the mid-1900s, had opinions on most people who ran the river. "Stinking!" he once shouted about Powell. "Awful! That man was a science, and if he had a brain in his head, after he got through the Green River, he would have built new boats. He pushed them through Grand Canyon, and he had a fine crew. But I don't see how he ever got as far as he did, to be honest with you."

Reilly, who died at 86 in 1996, had something to say about everyone's rowing style, and he gave reasons why some people wrecked their boats. His first vessels (he called them cataract boats) were pointed at both ends and boxy, with hardly any curve along the bottom and almost flat across the deck. When the river flowed at more than 127,000 cubic feet per second in 1957 — about 12 times what it is running on this day — Reilly's boats couldn't bear the force. In 1957, his boats were abandoned at Bright Angel Creek because they had lost too many oars. On a 1958 trip, at Lava Falls Rapid, the boats were shoved into the water and set free, as simple as letting go of a kite. Boats that cannot make the journey must be sacrificed, and in a number of places, discarded boats lie decaying on shore, left by the dead or the terrified or the humiliated. Reilly and his crew hiked out from there.

Reilly tried a third time in 1959, in the same boats, but the water was too rough. After repairs, the boats had patches on top of patches until they no longer would hold. Oars had again been broken and lost. Near Pipe Creek, Reilly filled the hatches of the boats with river stones. He punched openings in the hulls with a rock hammer and pushed the boats into the river, where they sank. Again, he walked away.

In 1962, Martin Litton proposed a different boat, and he talked Reilly into running the river again. Litton had been on the McKenzie River in Oregon, rowing a little fishing vessel called a drift boat. The thing had a bottom more curved than the runners of a rocking chair, and one of the sharpened ends pointed right up into the air.

Litton talked with a McKenzie boat builder and drew pictures of dories in the dirt. The boat builder supplied a couple of dories, and Reilly and Litton took them down the Colorado, 310 miles from above the Grand Canyon to its end. The trip took 20 days.

"Those were good boats," Reilly said. "They were a lot more maneuverable than the boats you're using today, I'll tell you that."

Hard-hulled boats such as skiffs and canoes take in too much water for a place like the Grand Canyon, with its rapid waves.

The dory has a different style of maneuverability and, although it bucks in the rapids like an animal trying to get something off its back, it tends to remain upright. As Reilly described it, you can get a dory to turn like a doorknob on an outhouse. And I have seen it — a man taking a dory to the top of a wave in the Grand Canyon, then screwing it in the opposite direction before falling off the back side.

These boats are about 16 1/2 feet long. There are no excesses to the dory's contours. Everything is refined for function. Entering a high wave, the bow cuts the water, but the river surface quickly comes in contact with the broad underside, forcing the dory to remain on the surface, rather than cut deeper. In this way, a dory adheres to the outline of the river and its currents. At the crest of a wave, a dory is thrown skyward. Canoes and kayaks, on the other hand, plunge through waves; rafts bend, sometimes in half.

Litton eventually collected a small fleet of dories and planned more of them with boat builder Jerry Briggs of Grants Pass, Oregon. Jerry Briggs had a way of combining a river and a vessel into a workable wooden shape. A sketch was made on paper and Briggs started building. The *Hidden Passage* is a Briggs boat, a result of about 100 years of boat evolution on the Colorado, and the mainstay of the Grand Canyon Dory company's fleet.

By the time these more sophisticated dories appeared, military rafts were being used to get down the river. Rubber pontoons were tied together, engines installed behind. People piled onto the inflated tubes and clutched at straps as they ran the rapids. As Litton says, "The disadvantage of the dory is that when you get to the end of the trip, you can't let the air out of it and roll it up in a ball and throw it in the back of a truck." There are other disadvantages: A raft hits a rock and there is a howling of rubber on stone, maybe a puncture and air whistling out like a blown tire. A dory hits a rock and splinters open.

EVENINGS SINK SO SLOWLY INTO the Canyon that you might not notice until it is too dark to read, and you are off somewhere, stumbling through rocks, heading back to camp. Dusk on the second night. Dories are lined along a slip of sand against the canyon wall. This is the only shore. The rest are planes of Redwall limestone meeting the river at sharp angles, and then the river moving solid as iron. There is not a place to get in or out of the Canyon. Even trying a walk up the only accessible tributary canyon, you will have to swim long passageways and climb, putting your forehead and bare toes against smooth, gray limestone. The canyon closes within a quarter-mile and you will stand there, shivering and wet, staring up curved archways that you cannot touch.

It has happened here: People going off the deep end early on a trip. Officially, it's called a "psychotic break." In lengthy and hazardous extractions, people have been helicoptered away, white knuckles clinging to the rescue litter. They didn't know, until they had come this far in, that they were being consumed by a canyon.

Tonight, people come to realizations in quiet ways. Brushing their teeth and looking up before spitting into the river, suddenly captivated by the view upcanyon, where the walls turn and close us in. Setting out gear, eating a meal, washing hands by the river. Everyone glances out at least once and is instantly taken. A passenger named Steve, who works on offshore drilling rigs near Singapore, tells me of a place he has found, something just downcanyon. In the morning, he walks me there. In his left hand he carries his coffee cup, in his right hand is a cigarette. He leads me along the beach where the cliff leans out as if it were about to fall.

The place is a grove of thick-leafed grasses green as asparagus. Sacred datura, tamarisk, a western redbud in bloom. He doesn't say "here it is" or gesture toward it. He just stops. It is not the Grand Canyon of typical picture

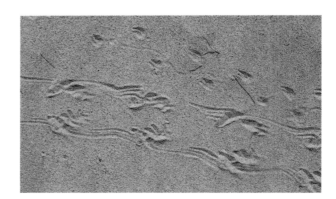

Top: In the shade of Redwall Cavern, boaters walk a sandy floor beneath a limestone ceiling at River Mile 33.

Tranquil
Moments

Left: A tiny dory floats the tranquil miles that end decisively at Lava Falls Rapids.

Above: Only a toad's tracks disrupt this beach.

books. It is a site, something very specific in all of this grandeur.

"So quiet," he says. "So beautiful." A drag off the cigarette. A blue-gray gnatcatcher flits through. I have to look closely to see that this small piece of ground is an orchestrated garden; one leaf over the next, an arrangement of light and dark, places where animals have troubled the grass. A hummingbird gathers itself on a limb, then whines away. The cigarette hangs between the man's fingers. All he can say, again, is "quiet and beautiful."

Third night. A fire of juniper driftwood. Monster shadows lift against the wall. A woman who rows one of the 18-foot supply rafts plays guitar and sings with a voice as sweet and modest as anything I've ever heard. Songs she wrote herself. It is when the talk of rapids is over, when the tired have gone to their sleeping bags, when each person is taken alone by whatever emotions come at night in the canyon.

Her voice carries to the river. Sounds of the guitar go a little further. Beyond that, our camp is only a trace of sound, replaced by the brush of wind and water mumbling for a couple of hundred miles. She continues singing, turning us all to ghosts around the fire.

At Nankoweap Canyon, morning clouds are windspun. White-throated swifts dust the sky. With their fleet spins and plummets, they appear to be gathering up the spindrift edges of clouds and fraying them into rain. We walk up slopes of boulders to the cliffs, and it is a cathedral of aeronautics. The swifts, belonging to the genus *Aeronautes*, slice the air into ribbons. They do tight circles, their wings shivering with speed, making the sound of wind across a wire.

Down at the river, I find an osprey wing washed onto the round cobbles by an eddy. The river brings these things: Stone. Wind. Feather. The rattle of arrowweed branches. The crescent curve of river sand at the beach.

We load into the dories — three or four passengers and one boatman to a dory, six dories all together — and follow the river. A storm comes down, clouds spilling from the Rim. They gather in the lee of Comanche Point, curling as if to sleep against the high cliff face. The Grand Canyon does this with storms, tears them apart and sows them across the landscape so that each canyon is planted with its own weather. Snow comes to within a couple of thousand feet of the river. Through rapids, we all cling to the gunwales, and river water rushes into our raingear, gripping our flesh.

IT NEEDS TO BE KNOWN THAT THE river is not the same as it was. There were people who brought boats here before 1963 who now would rather dance with a corpse than run the Colorado. You don't see many of them on the river any more; some are dead, others have too much pride.

Side canyons steadily muddy the river. The Little Colorado brings a reddish-brown silt that darkens

An osprey wing washed ashore.

the water, making the rapids appear hungrier. But here you will not feel heavy silt rasping against your boat, as you will higher on this river or on the Yampa, the San Juan, or the Green, all tributaries. Here, in the spring you will not be dodging dead cows or sheep, plastic oil bottles or tires, and floating mountains of trees in a river thick as slurry. That is a true desert river, one that garners all of the life and death and refuse of the land during runoff and sends it through a canyon.

Now Glen Canyon Dam captures the silt and flood debris that once would be here, impounding it in buried side canyons where houseboats drift overhead. The remains of eroding mountain ranges once came down this river, a quarter continent of mesas and slopes wearing into dust. Four hundred thousand tons of sediment on some days, 27 million tons on others. This was a river that recited verbatim the year's activities and the weight of snow in the mountains, in the spring rising to a feral red, for which the Spanish gave the Colorado its name, falling to an unnavigable trickle in the winter. In December, 1924, it ran at 700 cubic feet per second, 25 times lower than what it generally runs now. In the spring of 1884, it left high water marks suggesting a flow 20 times higher than today's flows.

To stabilize these fluctuations, a stair step of dams was planned to reach from the Mexican border through Nevada and Utah and as far as Colorado and Wyoming, making this the largest series of human-made lakes in the world. They would occupy not merely inner canyons, but the thousands of wandering tributaries. According to a 1946 report, "each dam would back reservoir water to the toe of the dam next upstream." Instead of peering off the Rim into an abyss, people would be looking into a quarter-filled Grand Canyon. You can see the test site tunnels and letters painted on rock walls, attesting to the ambition of dam planners.

In the early 1960s, Glen Canyon and its morsel of the Colorado River were dammed at the head of the Grand Canyon, partially to keep Lake Mead from filling with sediment, where 2 billion tons of silt already had collected in the slack waters, and partially to supply electricity to 2 million desert customers. Also, the dam was placed to regulate the river and gather some of its chaos into an accessible resource, regardless of how it increased evaporation rates of this stored river water. The newly impounded waters created a mecca for houseboats and cliff divers and bass fishermen and families from Ohio who otherwise would have not imagined they had reason to visit this desert.

Downstream, during peak working hours in Las Vegas and Phoenix, electricity demands keep the river running high through the turbines. Flows decrease on the weekends, bringing the river down, leaving parked rafts slopped like dirty laundry over newly exposed shoreline. The water is cold, about 47° F., taken from the chilled bottom of the reservoir. With the dam, the river became corporate. River running became a steady business, now depending on predictable flows so that the river's

personality could be easily memorized by boatmen. Without the dam, the river would be too wild to support the number of trips now running.

After Glen Canyon Dam's completion, there were plans for a Marble Canyon Dam that would take the upstream portion of the Grand Canyon. Martin Litton and his dories often are credited with holding back this project. Litton sat at a meeting of the Sierra Club board of directors the day the talk was of Marble Canyon Dam. The directors were about to back away from the fight if the Bureau of Reclamation agreed to install an elevator to transport people down to the trophy trout fishing in the clear tailrace waters.

Litton said, "Well, that sent me into a fit of rage and I stood up and expressed myself." His outburst swayed Sierra Club to abandon its support of the elevators and to fight against any dam ever suggested for the Canyon. Ads were taken out in *The New York Times.* Litton began shuttling people down the

Juniper, Juniperis ostrosperma

river in dories to get the word out. The Marble Canyon Dam plan collapsed.

Glen Canyon Dam, already constructed, closed its gates in 1963. It had not been built by evil men and women, but by people who wanted to feed the arid West and make a good American profit. They acted on their beliefs and, in doing so, piled billions of tons of sediment into a canyon where Powell once wrote: "Past these towering monuments, past these mounded billows of orange sand, past these oak-set glens, past these fern-decked alcoves, past these curves, we glided hour after hour . . ." Done by people not even born yet, those like myself, who would swim in the water and use the electricity of the impounded river.

Come down this river and you will have to remember Glen Canyon. Not just the Glen, but its side canyons in the grim, careless dark of Lake Powell — Twilight Canyon, Dungeon Canyon, Music Temple, Cathedral Canyon, Dark Canyon, Balanced Rock Canyon, Warm Spring Canyon, Hidden Passage, Ticaboo Canyon. Listing these names is not meant to rally your anger. I offer them because knowledge of a river cannot be severed by what happens to a particular canyon or a geographic name or by the creation of a dam and its reservoir. The knowledge of a river must be long and complete, and the Grand Canyon is neither a beginning nor an end. It is a gesture along the path of moving water.

I AM IN THE NIPOMO DUNES ON A run with Shawn Browning, who has been down this river more than 50 times. He lets me sit on the point of the bow, my legs hanging off either side, and then he takes me into the throat of a rapid, burying me to my shoulders in a wave. Shawn is a combination of trickery and sweetness, the way he grins so wisely, how he plays the river like a canyon wren flirting among boulders. He will row hard to get up front, then stop and cradle hands behind his head, letting his dory drift sideways while the boatmen just behind have to work out of his path. He runs a Butler boat, from a limited edition of long, wide, high-riding dories built by Paul Butler in Montana.

Shawn owns this boat; bought it from Grand Canyon Dories after he wrecked it in Lava Falls. He struck a rock just as a wave smacked inside the center of the boat. The dory twisted along its axis, causing the entire deck to separate and collapse. Shawn offered cash to take it off the company's hands. He fixed it up and got it back on the river. I've seen him in the warehouse with it, sanding the wooden grips by hand, talking about how she doesn't like being off the river for long.

Days grow warmer and snow on the Rim melts. The river's surface is graced with galaxies of whirlpools. Vishnu schist rises from the floor and the Canyon pinches in. Rapids become huge, driven by industrial hydraulics, by great volumes of water thundering into narrow hallways. This is not a classic white water river with dangerous rapids cropping up at every rock. Here, many of the rocks are buried under a mass of water.

A lot has been said about the rapids of the Grand Canyon. They are, indeed, intimidating, these massive muscular knots of water kicking up shadows that can be seen from the Rim thousands of feet above. But this river is more of a float than an insane ride. It is more of a

slow tour through a canyon than a screaming plunge into oblivion. Of course, to be in a dory on the fifth wave at Hermit Rapids, which looks like a billowing circus tent, or to funnel down the tongue of Horn Creek Rapids, is like teasing a giant.

We scout Granite Rapids. The guides stand there on a boulder in the sun, waving their arms at the white water. The rapids are too bony with rocks on the left, where it sometimes can be cheated, so we have to run right. The right side of Granite always is a big ride.

I am with Roger Dale in the *Roaring Springs*. Roger collects spare change in his footwell; it is luck to keep from dumping. Last time he flipped was in Marble Canyon. Sheared off an oarlock, lost the right gunwale and the entire bowpost, as well as the change in his footwell. Today, he carries 16 cents: a penny, a dime, and a nickel. He is one of the people who howls in a rapid, who takes the wild runs and puts your head right over the big holes. But I have seen him at night by the fire. I've seen his eyes turn soft as he stares away. Off the river, he is a glass blower, and I have noticed in his gallery work the same curves you see at the entrance to a rapid. For all the gristle and chaos of white water, he seems to know that the beauty lies in the smooth water at the head.

At the top of Granite Rapids, the water swells, then slopes inside. All eddies and whirlpools are drawn tight. We sail across this tongue, where the gradient of the water and the underside of the boat adhere to the same mathematical constant. Just below the dory, the rapid inhales, and it looks like you could lose a boat in there. This is a moment of beauty, the run of the dory just before the rupture of the first wave, before the oars are pounded back,

before the river slams against the deck. This is the sweet curve of power, the water taut as a drum head. I hold my breath as we cross.

Everything after that is impact and gritted teeth. Ten or 15 seconds. Fast work on the oars. Then free, spinning, slinging water out with bailing scoops. Roger shouting like a madman.

I once came across an oral interview with P.T. Reilly, made four years before his death. I put on headphones and listened to him talk about high water and the lousy stink of commercial outfits. He talked about the sound of boulders rolling in the river the year he had to abandon his boats.

"When Boulder Narrows is completely covered," he said, "and that hole down below — boy, if anything gives you the holy shakes, that hole at the downstream side of Boulder Narrows would do it. Damn thing; you could drop a cottonwood tree in there and it would go out of sight."

I listened to his tapes to hear the voice of a dead river runner, to listen for water in his speech. I wanted to know what the river trips were like for him. He never spoke highly of those who made

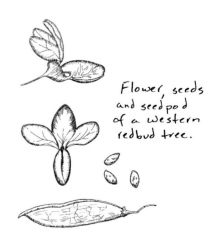

Flower, seeds and seed pod of a western redbud tree.

money running the river, people like Norm Nevills or Georgie White. "Georgie," he said. "That old wretch. [Her group] went swimming in the pool at Elves Chasm and we saw cigar butts in there and they put pennies and nickels and dimes. I even found a quarter in there. Trash in there. It was horrible! It was really rank."

He talked slowly, pausing between phrases. He sounded old, cantankerous. But not angry. The trips he ran were simple. Only in 1962 did he carry an ice box for fresh meat. "We had steaks the first two or three nights. I think one of my prize dinners was about a mile above Vasey's. There's a little cove on the left I call Redbud Camp. Lot of redbud trees there; a lot of dead redbud trees. And that makes wonderful broiling for steaks. Redbud wood."

In those days, Reilly took anybody down, whoever could produce enough cash for him to break even. It wasn't a business. By the early 1960s, only about 300 people, including John Wesley Powell, had ever run the Colorado River through the Grand Canyon.

Reilly returned to the river in the 1980s, when tens of thousands of people were going down each year, and he was

saddened by the sight. "Too many people run the river. They don't know beans about it. All they want to do . . . [they've seen it on TV or something] and they want to say, 'Oh, I've run the Grand Canyon.' But they don't know anything about it. I've always thought, unless you've been a boatman and felt the surge of the river on the oars, that you don't really get the full significance of it anyway."

He said that businesses just keep people moving, charging thousands of dollars a person, offering extravagant meals, helicopter rides, volleyball nets on the beach — drop people off, then turn around and get the next trip out. He probably was right, but I am weighing his words against these boatmen I know, these people with hands on oars.

In 1988, Grand Canyon Dories sold out to a larger raft company. Litton was losing money, and he had to back out. He hadn't wanted the thing to become a business anyhow.

The dory group did not stay for the money ($80 to $100 a day is the going rate for a skilled dory guide in the Canyon). They took pay cuts and held on with their fingernails because it was the Canyon, the river, and the community.

Meanwhile, the nature of the business changed around them. It used to be that the edges of these companies were rough. Stories told are

outlandish, seat-of-the-pants outfits giving clients the rides of their lives. Now, the edges are now being sanded smooth by legality, liability, and regulations. Coconino County expects restaurant standards during food preparation on the river, and an inspector is sent down for surprise visits. The county health department would like hair nets to be worn in the river kitchen and for chlorine to be added to drinking water. Companies struggle to hold onto their insurance as lawsuits cloud the air, so that now it makes more sense to stack people side-by-side on a motor rig than to get off a small boat and hike a steep side canyon as far as you can go, then go a little further. The drunken, dangerous days of guiding have been bankrupted.

Still, I weigh the changes against the integrity of these people running the river. Elena Kirschner curls her body over a watercolor pad, and only when I offer my own journal sketches does she allow me to see hers. Jan Kempster carries passengers in the *Animas*, a dory she took a year and a half to build with her own hands. Katherine MacDonald leads people on a hike, up a dark chimney in which we all wedge flesh against rock to get to the top — where she can show us the blooms of purple sage. Bronco waits for me, walking down a side canyon, and when I stop beside him, he points at an Anasazi handprint painted on the wall, says nothing, and walks away.

These are the people who now belong to the river, people who read and drink and live this water. They are not Reilly. They are not Litton. It is not the same river. These are not the same boats. But this arrangement of baffling cross-currents and high waves demands the same reflexes. The river has little concern

Detail of an oar in its oarlock

The
Weather
Intrudes

Right: Boaters pull their dories up on the wet but only unflooded floor at the rear of Redwall Cavern during the record Colorado River flows in 1983.

Below: Geologists load their raft after a September rain conjures up fog, enchanting the Colorado River and haunting the Kaibab Suspension Bridge.

for a person's physical strength or stature. It is the sparseness of motions that matters.

When dory guides talk about those they admire, they refer to the amount of time the oars are left out of the water, to the heedfulness of each move and the reading of the river. This kind of knowledge seldom is learned on television or in textbooks or by story-telling. This knowledge involves the pressure of water against an oar blade, and then the pressure of oar against the hand. The tying of a good tautline hitch. The place where clear water can be gathered for the evening meal. The angle of a bow taken into a strong eddy.

Late in the day, below the apricot glow of Redwall cliffs, the dories are scattered in Muav Gorge. If any sunlight gets down here this time of day, it is well tarnished. Shields of limestone, decorated with terraces and spires, surround us. When the river turns slightly to the north, all the cliffs close on each other like books slammed shut. The river looks as if it ends here. We tie off to shore. Most people find napping holes in the sand while a few of us sling on day packs and crawl through the knife edges of weathered limestone. This is a random hike, a choice to stop here, a crack of a side canyon we would have easily passed without taking note. It is too steep and immediate for a trail or a name. It is just a place.

The canyon is a hollow of toppled boulders. Bighorn sheep have been here, leaving droppings and tracks. We climb the fine handholds, under the stained-glass shade of western redbud leaves. We follow each other across accidental stone bridges and up the smooth scours of flash floods. The back of the canyon lifts like a hand, stopping us.

The bighorn sheep go on from here. They must take these finite ledges on the east wall, skirting to higher levels. I climb as far as I can, to the prow of the canyon, where springs seep from under plumes of maidenhair ferns. I shift my feet so that I can crouch on a slanted surface, leaning against a hanging boulder. I look down. Six people lounge on boulders, lying in the shade the way snakes lie in the sun. Anyone makes a sound, and we all hear it. A hand brushed against rock. A long breath taken out of pleasure. In the back, water drips from a small vault that would perfectly hold a statue of the Virgin of Guadalupe and a hundred years of offerings scattered at her feet. Water taps on rock, sounds like the last drops of a rain storm. These "shrines" are bundled into the rocks; there are so many along the Grand Canyon that they cannot be counted. These are the places that build the Canyon — places mostly unseen.

In the morning, Katherine has a sponge in her hand and works steadily, cleaning the inside and outside of the dory *Ticaboo* as if she expected guests. I sit in the sand and talk to her about superstition, about the spare change Roger keeps in his footwell, and about why Elena won't wear the shirt she wore the day she flipped in Nevills Rapids. Katherine scrubs out every bit of sand as we talk, then scrubs it out again.

Today we will run Lava Falls. It is not the most dangerous and certainly not the most technical. But it is big and has a reputation. It is a noble thing to flip in Lava. Still, everyone wants some gravity against a bad run. Katherine is the only guide here who has not capsized in Lava, but, at 27, she also is the youngest and has made the fewest runs. When she first came here, she was a trainee on a raft for another company. While scouting Lava Falls, her boatman turned to her and informed her that she would be on the oars for this rapid. Katherine had to walk away for a moment; she almost vomited.

Just before noon, I stand behind her as she scouts Lava Falls. At the brink, sounds of moving water fold over one another like origami; there is no way to trace the origin of a single noise. Beneath the high-pitched sounds of waves that break their own backs is a baritone rumble stirring the basement of the earth. It is the sound of fear.

The rapid looks like the river turned inside out, so that all of its muscles and bones poke through. Once a boat is in the rapid, there is little that can be done with the oars. Some boatmen just let go of the oars and sprawl across the deck, trying to hold the boat down. What is inside of this particular rapid is mostly luck. Of all the skill and years spent on the river, all the careful maneuvers and strength against oars and reading of water, it is luck. A dory once flipped seven times before exiting Lava. Another time, an unoccupied commercial raft got loose during the night and floated the river. In the morning it was found upright in an eddy below Lava Falls. Eggs that had been left on the deck were still in place.

Because Lava Falls is so much luck, the boat people are afraid to say too much about it. Words might matter. Certain rules are held between these people, nothing cultish or standardized, just unspoken acts. When happenstance might easily undermine a person's skill — say, in farming, hunting, or running rivers — you will find personal ceremonies. To keep the frost from coming early, to prevent the wind from broadcasting your scent, to hold your boat upright through the lateral waves. There is no way to measure the significance of simple, ritualistic gestures, even if it is only the wearing of gaudy, colored shorts brought out just for Lava. But they could count. A mile upstream of Lava Falls, a 60-foot anvil of basalt stands in the river. It is the gateway. Prayers are made to this rock. Hands touch it as people pass, the way one scatters offerings at the feet of Buddha. Not long ago, oblations were common here. Coins were thrown onto the crags, curious objects of sacrifice, such as little troll dolls, were left on ledges. Ask most river runners what they left at the rock and they just grin sheepishly.

A complaint once arrived at the Park Service from Hualapai Indians who were ashamed to see these offerings. It was asked that objects no longer be left. Religions quietly clashed at this rock. The request carried the weight of tradition, coming long before dories and before people who find sanctity in running a river. But the boatmen are now the subjects of this river, those who depend on the kindness of destiny or chance or gods. The request was respected by river runners, and the trinkets were removed from the monolith. But you still find some river stones up there — smooth, round

objects of nature placed within reach of a boat.

We are taking the left run in Lava Falls. At the commonly low water levels, this left route was not available. But a debris flow spilled from the nearest side canyon in March, 1995, rearranging the left side and adding a bit more energy to the right. A science crew had been camped nearby the night the debris flow came down with a flash flood. In the morning the rapid was impossible to run. Flood-driven rocks nearly plugged the river. The crew spent hours milling through the debris, not taking measurements, just staring. By the end of that day, the debris had been reworked by the river, and this new left passage was beginning to show. Prior to that, the usual routes were far right or through the slot next to the ledge hole.

Bronco goes first in the *Phantom*, then Elena. As soon as the starting line

at the top is hit, the dories are gone. The undersides of their sterns flash once in the sunlight, and then, some seconds later, I can see a bow jabbed straight up like a spear hurled into the air. Then an oar blade barely visible. Otherwise, nothing can be seen.

Nothing can be seen until Katherine leans hard against the oars and the river falls out from under us. I am in the stern, the only one back here. As we drop, I am lifted. For a quarter-second, I can see the entire rapid. We tumble inside and are pounded to the right. Too far right. The dory cocks on edge and we all leap to the high side, clinging to the gunwale to keep from going over. We almost crawl onto the bottom of the dory. Out of the corner of my eye, I see Katherine's leg against the sky. A wave has thrown her clear of the

A dory inside of Lava Falls Rapids.

boat. Without anyone on them, the oars wrack against their locks.

There is no canyon to be seen. Just haystacks of water and an empty space where Katherine had been. The last thing on earth I want to do is jump into the footwell and grab the oars. I imagine, in the short time I have to imagine, myself snatching the oars and finding myself bearing straight down on that big black rock on the right. (I've heard enough stories about that rock. A dory called *Lava Cliff* once was lost in the eddy just above it.) The oars slam around, chewed by monsters below.

Katherine drags like a spinning lure, her left arm clamped to the boat where she has grabbed one of the deck straps. She does not look afraid. She looks like an animal trying not to be eaten. Her blonde hair is going everywhere in the water. We crash down from the wave and, when the dory levels for a second, a wave surges in from the left. Katherine and a large amount of water slosh square into the footwell. Her right hand instantly grabs an oar.

Katherine is in. The oars are in her hands. A wall of water comes down. It packs up my nose, into my sinuses, inside my ears. The dory heaves up the next wave. There is a free-fall instant between impacts, a turning of the stomach. One oar grabs at the air.

Then we are out. We slide into an eddy and in the middle of bailing, Katherine, who is burning with electricity, tells the two men in the bow that she had been thrown out of the dory. She grins when she says this. They think she is kidding. "No," I shout. "She was gone, she was out of the boat."

THE CEILING OF THE WAREHOUSE IN Flagstaff is a museum of busted dories, with shattered bows and transoms hung and nailed to the rafters. The bow of the *Emerald Mile* and of the *Music Temple* are up there. Stories are left dangling all over the place.

Stored on a far wall are the fresh hulls of two dories, their decks not yet built, names not yet given. These boats are a foot and a half longer and 10 inches wider at the oarlocks than the Briggs boats. There is a bit more rocker along the bottom to improve pivoting. The flat Briggs transom at the stern is replaced by a pointed end. They are not made of wood.

The problem with many boats damaged in the Canyon is that, after repairs, river water lingers inside of the plywood. The hulls rot from the inside out, and the warehouse is haunted with the dust of constant major hull repairs. Considering the effects of Glen Canyon Dam on sediment transport, there is less sand and more rock in the Canyon every season. Dories pulled to shore are gouged by these rocks, necessitating more repairs. Thus, more rotting wood.

So the next generation of dories is made of core cell foam instead of marine plywood. One guide tells me that buoyancy is altered, that she can feel slight differences when a dory without wood is in the water. Another says that they are the same. I once asked the company manager, who sat in an office adjoining the warehouse, about dories without wood. He runs dories himself. His wife and his three brothers run dories. He said that the foam is more expensive, but it will pay for itself. It seemed fanciful to

suggest he stay with wood, considering the cost of things, so I only asked about it once. I didn't want to sound ridiculous — or sentimental.

FOR THE LAST COUPLE OF HUNDRED miles, the Grand Canyon has opened and closed like a bird testing its wings. In places, it seemed no wider than a door left slightly open, the highest rims separated by only 600 yards. Then the Canyon would spread, 18 miles from rim to rim, unveiling a night full of stars. In the open, fractured land of the Hurricane Fault we walked to a ridge and it seemed as if there — with broad farewell views to the far rims — the Grand Canyon would make a graceful completion. Instead, within minutes of us rowing below Diamond Creek, the Canyon snapped shut like a trap and buried us again.

In these miles, the Canyon has been boastfully vast, then as intimate as a quiet conversation. It has been ruled by Redwall limestone, then by the glassy tiles of Dox sandstone, then by the Roman-pillar architecture of recently spilled lava.

A canyon tree frog,
Hyla arenicolor.

Scouting at Requiem Rapids, Mile 232, I am wandering in the Vishnu schist where the river has carved the place into skeletons. While the guides congregate at the river, talking about the fangs on the right side and how to avoid them, I am lost in this gallery of impossibly erotic shapes. The rock is as smooth as polished oak. Look at it one way, the place is sculpture; another way, it is a grid of mathematics, showing hydrologic qualities of high river water. Hoops are inside of hoops, archways leading into chambers that flare like fine glasswork. Trace the inside of one of these hollows with your fingers and it is like feeling the crescent moon. Some of the smaller protrusions, flanges so fine they might easily break, show where whirlpools have rubbed against one another. The river is like this for miles.

There are only two customers left from the original 24 who began at Lees Ferry. Many opted for the helicopter ride out at Whitmore Wash a couple of days ago. Others hiked out at Phantom Ranch in the middle. What they are not seeing is Lower Granite Gorge, the final 50 miles of the Canyon. Tombstone faces of Redwall can be seen over the darkened schist cliffs. The rapids become loud and the river coils into multi-faceted eddies. Waterfalls descend gowns of travertine, one working itself into a canyon that looks like a cave, with dangling swaths of flowstone and ribboned stalactites.

On the last night, we tie the rafts and dories together into a single mass. Now we are on Lake Mead, which has backed into the gorge. The water turns sluggish. The rapids, one being the largest in the entire Canyon, are buried and the surface does not even stir. Martin Litton took his original commercial trips to Lake Mead so that he could show people what a reservoir-flooded Grand Canyon would look like. Not just a small portion is under water, but about 36 miles of it. The winding slots of tributary canyons are down there, underneath.

A two-cycle engine is attached to a metal frame on the flotilla, but it is not started right away. We push off in the dark, taking whatever oars are available to position ourselves within the Canyon. No flashlights are turned on. There is no moon. Only a blizzard of stars. As we drift, someone up front plays a flute. Sound is taken into the cliffs; scraps of echoes drift down on us. I make a bed on the deck of the *Phantom* and sleep at the gunwales where I can occasionally reach over and drag my fingers through the water.

Dawn. I am sitting up in my bag. Elena anchored us here at about 2:30 this morning. I try to wake myself quickly so nothing looks groggy through my morning eyes. The Grand Canyon holds its staggering posture, even this close to the end. The engine is roused with a pull cord, and I remain sitting in my bag. Up to the last moment, great side canyons are ushered in. A waterfall descends a southeast canyon, truncated as it hits the reservoir.

Then, within a mile, the Grand Canyon ceases and we are deposited in an unfamiliar land. The sky opens like a parachute. The entire Canyon ends. Just like that.

From what I saw of this canyon in the last several weeks, I filled an 80-page notebook, then ran out of space and had to write in all of the margins. An entire nation of canyons lies behind me. Blocky ridges and low hills appear in the distance. The formations of the Grand Canyon — Coconino, Muav limestone, Bright Angel shale — are taken into the earth, broken by the alien Basin and Range Province into fill dirt.

I once talked with a geologist about changes to the rapids in the Grand Canyon. Being very fond of processes, he'd studied the alignment of boulders and how floods shifted certain ones into place and moved others out. He was there for the last debris flow at Lava Falls, witnessed a new whirlpool blossoming on the right side. With all of their maddening details, rapids will never reinvent themselves. He submitted his arm straight out when he said this, making a line with this gesture. Everything moves forward and does not return.

The designs of certain boats are abandoned. Canyons are carved into regions once as smooth as a Kansas plain. River runners die, along with their ways of cooking with redbud wood. I sometimes pray that old ways might remain. That the boats would always be wooden and that the river would again, soon, run mad with spring floods. But nothing has permanent residence here. In a few months, the cloudbursts of summer will return, as they did when I arrived last summer, sending flash floods and boulders to the river, working these thousands of canyons into new shapes.

The engine drones behind me. Our flotilla bends the mirrored surface of Lake Mead and I breathe the changed air, trying to remember a place as rich and evanescent as a lucid dream.

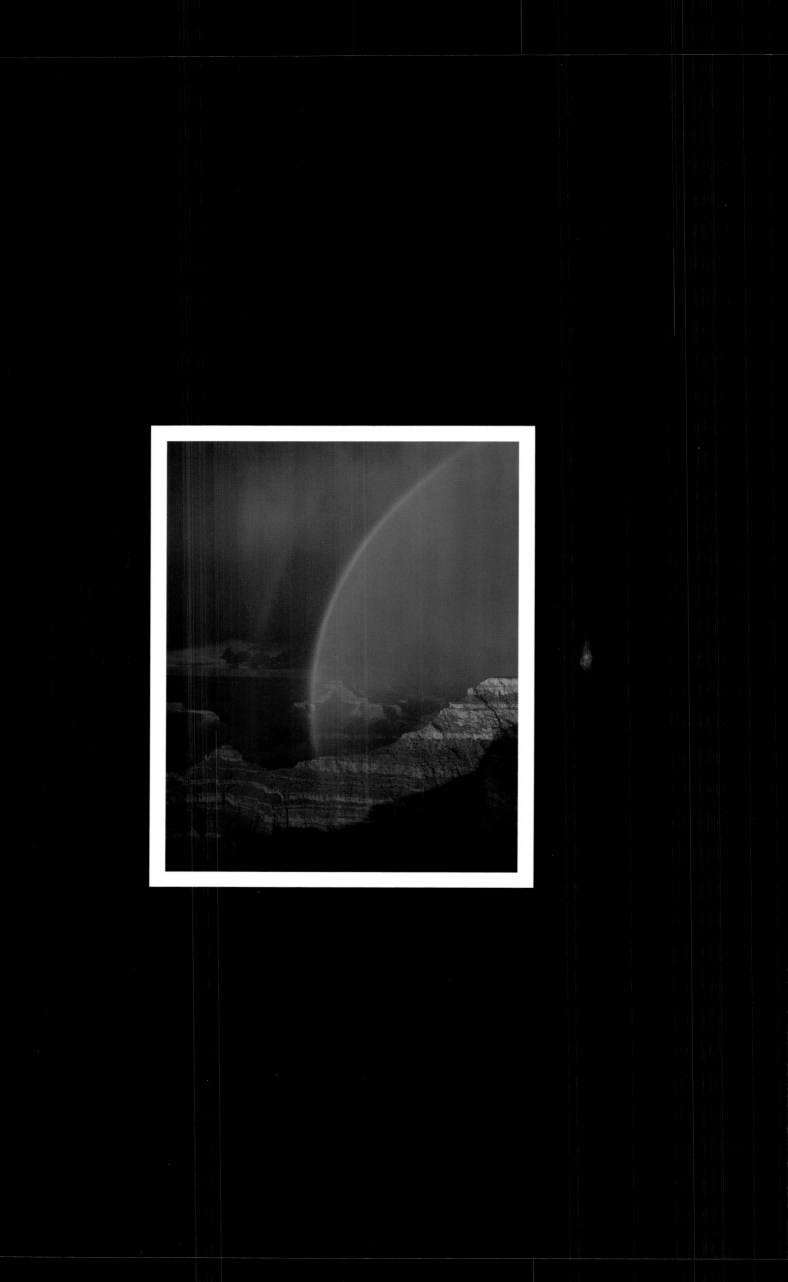

RHYTHMS AND CYCLES

GREAT DRAMA EXUDES FROM THE RHYTHMS AND CYCLES OF THE CENTURIES.
WITHIN THIS FRAMEWORK EMERGE ENDLESS TRANSITIONS AND IMAGES.

Each day, cliff shadows trace open arcs on the sand and bedrock. Each week, sunrise and sunset describe new courses and destinations. The months fine tune the colors of cottonwoods, mesquites, and willows. Each year assumes the uniqueness of a flower, its general design familiar but its lines, textures, and tones varying in nuance.

Centuries bring rockfalls and floods, each a modest rearrangement of the Canyon furniture. Boulders shift, trees topple, and deltas expand then wither away. Temperatures, cloud formations, vegetation patterns, rain, snow, and droughts produce an endless combination of conditions overlaying Canyon topography.

In the monsoon season — July and August — the Colorado River almost hourly recasts its color as each tributary canyon spills its own unique brew of mud, gravel, logs, and unlucky rabbits into the torrent. In the fluctuating flows, in the textures and tints of the creamy muds, and in the evolving patterns of ripple marks, complex and beautiful worlds are designed and destroyed overnight.

Because of rhythms and cycles, you never know what you will find when plunging through a rapid or entering an intimate grotto. The changes since your previous visit can be whimsical, heartbreaking, or staggering. Most of the time, they attract little notice, lost in a larger atmosphere of wonder.

The seasons, too, add blankets of snow on the plateaus, color in the aspens, fog on the river, dark clouds pouring out over the precipices.

With evolving atmospheric displays, seasonal colors, plant changes, migrations, climate wobbles, and geologic reshuffling, the enduring Grand Canyon is hardly immutable. It shimmers with unfolding variances.

Especially on land along the Rim, every passing month leaves its imprint: the mists and snows of January and February, the crazy weather of March, the flowers of April and May, the clear skies and northern sunrises and sunsets of June, the thunderstorms of July and August, the turning colors of September and October, and the punctuated slide into winter with the coming of November and December.

All this molds into a feast of change, large and small, on the rims and in the corridors of Grand Canyon.

In the words of Immanuel Kant, "Creation is always busy making new scenes, new things, and new Worlds."

Opposite: An August rainbow arcs into the Canyon in a view from Mather Point on the South Rim. Such sights occur frequently during Arizona's summer storm season, also called "monsoon" season.

Opposite: Claret cup hedgehog blooms as best it
can in a chilling rain in
late April in Jumpup
Canyon on the
Canyon's north side.

Bouquets in the
Rocks

Above: Near the
mouth of Sowats
Canyon, pepperweed
brightens a stormy day.

Life and Death

Left: On the Esplanade below Sowats Point, waterpockets dot the sandstone benches.

Right: The stalks of agaves stand as sentinels nearly a year after their deaths near Forster Canyon.

Below: Redbud limbs bend beneath the weight of purple bouquets in the narrows of Jumpup Canyon.

Opposite: The flowering of prickly pear cactus gladdens grassy benches along the Little Colorado River.

Summer in Side Canyons

Above: Agaves protect their space on a rocky shelf near River Mile 120.

Right: In the sheltered confines of Saddle Canyon, a modest community of trees, shrubs, and grasses prepares for summer heat.

Following panel: Morning sunlight pours into Marble Gorge at River Mile 41 at the mouth of Buck Farm Canyon.

Clear Days of June

Autumn Aspens Ablaze

Top: Aspens catch the brilliance of fall on the east-facing slopes below Marble Viewpoint in early October.

Above: Along the North Kaibab Trail, a canopy of aspens lights the way.

Right: A conflagration of shimmering yellow aspens rages at the edge of the Kaibab Plateau at Marble Viewpoint.

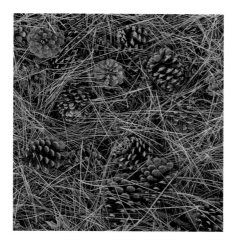

Left: Lengthening shadows radiate from the forest trees near East Rim Viewpoint in October.

Winter Approaches

From top: Ponderosa pine needles and cones litter the forest floor near Cape Royal, ensuring trees for the future.

An aspen leaf turns yellow, its autumn color.

An oak leaf glows crimson.

Above: At Soap Creek Rapids in early February. Few river runners float the Colorado River in mid-winter.

Winter Down in the Canyon

Opposite: Boulders warm themselves in the late January sun near Salt Water Wash, River Mile 12.

Following panel: Sunrise comes late in January. Viewed from Yaki Point, O'Neill Butte turns incandescent, illuminating an inner Canyon still lost in the subdued light of dawn.

Snow Below the Rim

Opposite: January clouds play along the North Rim, viewed from Yaki Point on the South Rim.

Fog, Mists, and Silent Nights

Above: Fog shrouds the South Rim near Mather Point, while Wotans Throne and Vishnu Temple scrape the clouds in the distance.

Right: Mists drift through the ponderosa pine forest near Yaki Point in early March.

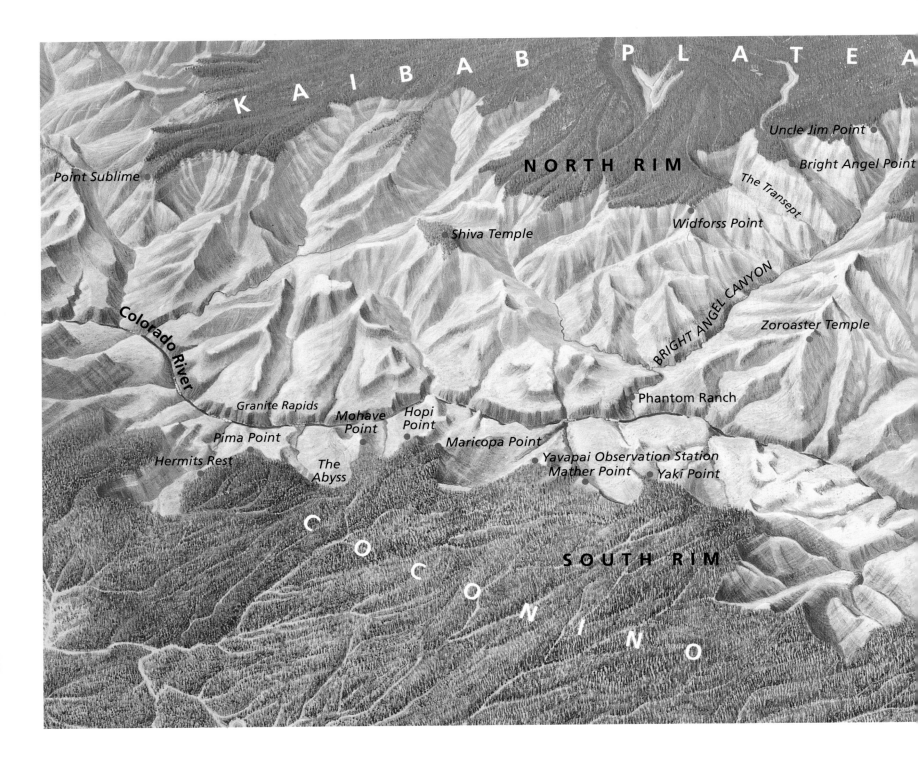

GRAND CANYON NATIONAL PARK

The map at right, prepared by National Park Service cartographers, covers virtually all of the 277-mile length of the Grand Canyon. Approximately one-third of the map, beginning at the right edge, is covered in Robert Tope's illustration based on topographic maps. His work relates a sense of the inner Canyon — the hundreds of canyons and side canyons that lie below the rims of the Grand Canyon.

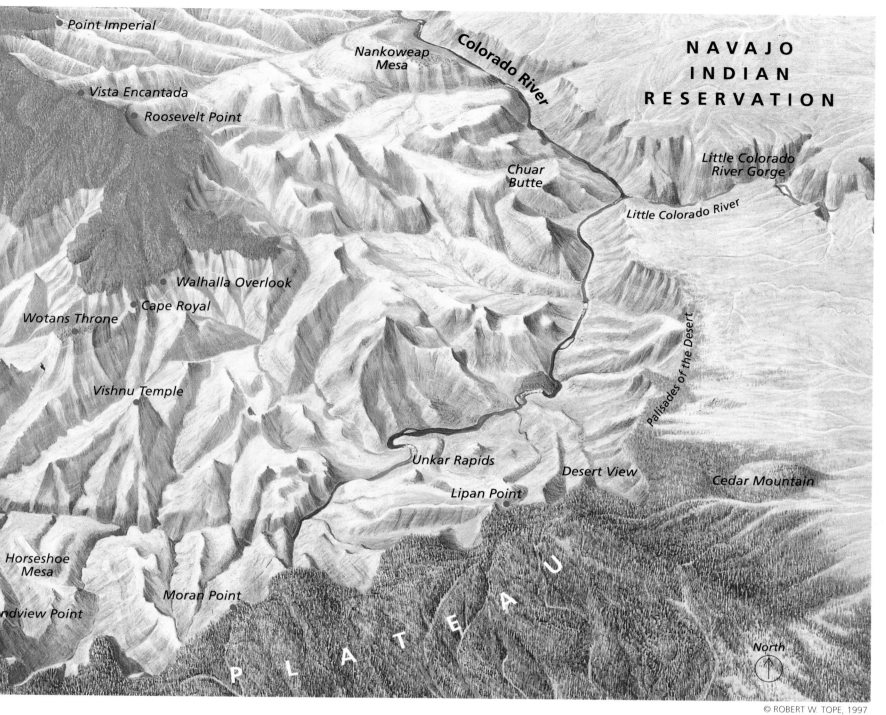

© ROBERT W. TOPE, 1997

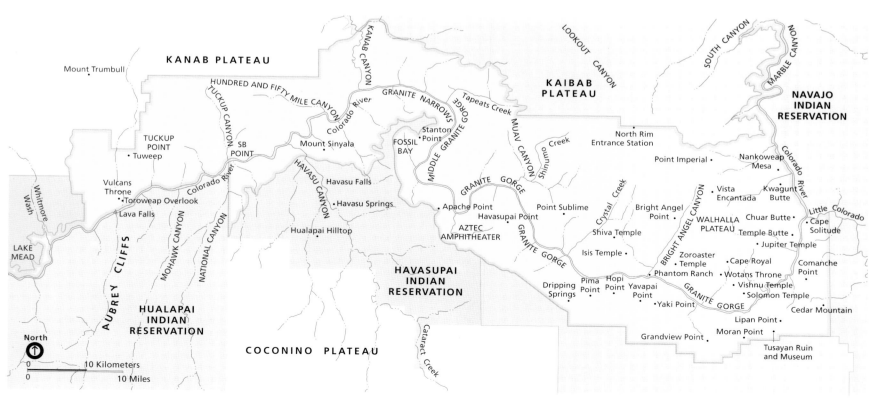

INDEX OF PHOTOGRAPHS AND ILLUSTRATIONS

Page numbers in boldface type denote illustrations.